Information Systems Engineering Library

Prototyping in an SSADM Environment

Janet Blowers O'Neill

CCTA

February 1993

LONDON: HMSO

004 .21 RT

© Crown Copyright 1993

Applications for reproduction should be made to HMSO

First published 1993

ISBN 0 11 330582 6
ISSN 0967-9561

For further information regarding this publication and other CCTA products please contact:

Library
Riverwalk House
157-161 Millbank
London SW1P 4RT

071-217-3331

Contents

Foreword

1 Introduction   1

    1.1 Purpose

    1.2 Who should read this volume

    1.3 Structure of this volume

2 Overview   3

    2.1 What is prototyping?

    2.2 Environment for prototyping

    2.3 Management of prototyping

    2.4 SSADM and prototyping

3 Introduction to prototyping   7

    3.1 What is meant by prototyping?

    3.2 Why use prototyping?

    3.3 Risks of prototyping

    3.4 When to use prototyping within SSADM

4 Environmental factors   17

    4.1 User commitment

    4.2 IT required skills

    4.3 Tools

    4.4 Other environmental factors

5	**Management of prototyping**	27
	5.1 Project staffing	
	5.2 Estimating	
	5.3 Prototype planning	
	5.4 Negotiation	
	5.5 Managing prototyping sessions	
	5.6 Evaluation of user feedback	
	5.7 Control of prototyping	
	5.8 Documentation	
6	**SSADM and prototyping**	45
	6.1 Feasibility Study module	
	6.2 Requirements Analysis module	
	6.3 Requirements Specification module	
	6.4 Logical System Specification module	

Annexes   71

Annex A   Possible prototyping tools

Annex B   Estimating approaches

Bibliography   89

Glossary   91

Foreword

The **Information Systems Engineering Library** provides guidance on carrying out Information Systems Engineering activities. In the IS life cycle, Information Systems Engineering takes place once the IS strategy has been defined. It is concerned with the development of information systems up to the operational stage, when an information system becomes the responsibility of infrastructure management.

The Information Systems Engineering Library builds on the guidance in the CCTA IS Guides B set: *Systems Development Set* and complements other CCTA products, in particular the IS project management method, PRINCE, and the systems analysis and design method, SSADM.

The Information Systems Engineering Library is of interest to IS providers, helping them to improve the quality and productivity of their IS development work. It may be of interest to business managers, whose business operations depend on having effective IS support by means of Information Systems Engineering activities.

CCTA welcomes customer views on Information Systems Engineering Library publications. Please send your comments to:

Customer Services
Information Systems Engineering Group
Gildengate House
Upper Green Lane
Norwich NR3 1DW

Acknowledgements

The assistance of Richard Smith (BIS) and CMG, under contract to CCTA, is gratefully acknowledged.

1 Introduction

1.1 Purpose

Prototyping helps users participate in the analysis and design of information systems and take ownership of those systems. It is a valuable technique when used in the right circumstances and with the right approach. The purpose of this volume is to help practitioners to identify both the circumstances and the approach and to show how prototyping can be used as part of the Structured Systems Analysis and Design Method (SSADM) activity.

Prototyping should be viewed as a highly effective tool for the use of the SSADM practitioner. This volume describes the benefits of prototyping and explains when the technique can be used with SSADM. It also shows that prototyping is not a substitute for the analysis tasks but is an additional analysis technique within the SSADM framework.

This volume does more than indicate the technical activities carried out in prototyping. It describes the factors that must be taken into account when deciding to use prototyping and the management approach to be taken to plan and control the process. These considerations are vital to the success of prototyping.

The types of prototyping covered by this volume are:

- Demonstration
- Requirements
- Specification, extended beyond the coverage in the SSADM Reference Manuals
- Research.

1.2 Who should read this volume

This volume is intended for Information Technology (IT) application development managers, systems analysis and design managers, IT development project managers or team leaders, SSADM practitioners and users who are to have parts of their IT system prototyped.

1.3 Structure of this volume

Chapter 2 provides an overview to this volume.

Chapter 3 defines prototyping and discusses the benefits and risks associated with it.

Chapter 4 discusses the environmental factors.

Chapter 5 describes project management of prototyping.

Chapter 6 covers the methods and techniques for each type of prototyping together with details of interfaces to SSADM.

Annex A covers the possible prototyping tools that may be used.

Annex B discusses the estimating approaches that may be used.

2 Overview

Prototyping can help to improve the effectiveness of information system development in the right circumstances. It enhances communication between users and developers. It is a tool to help developers share the user's understanding of the business processes the IS/IT system is planned to support. For the user, it increases their understanding and involvement in the analysis and design process so that they can actually help discover the right solution. This helps to ensure that:

- the proposed system meets business needs
- users take ownership of their system
- organisational impact is identified and managed throughout the process.

Successful prototyping cannot be achieved simply by employing a prototyping tool (see section 4.3 Tools). Success requires the right technical tools, users, IT staff skills and the right management approach.

2.1 What is prototyping?

In this volume, prototyping is defined as the *development of a preliminary version of part, or all, of a software system to allow various aspects of that system to be investigated*. A prototype is used to obtain feedback from the intended users. This feedback is reflected in the analysis and design, increasing user confidence in the final system. A prototype can be used to investigate problem areas or the implications of other options.

There are a number of reasons why prototyping may prove beneficial in a system development:

- clarification of requirements
- gaining user commitment
- improving developer understanding
- speeding up the development process
- verification of designs

- automation of specifications
- checking feasibility
- elicitation of requirements.

The following types of prototyping are discussed in this volume:

- Demonstration Prototyping
- Requirements Prototyping
- Specification Prototyping
- Research Prototyping.

2.2 Environment for prototyping

In Chapter 4, the following aspects within which prototyping is to operate are described:

- the amount and nature of user commitment needed, given that prototyping demands a greater involvement from the user
- the skills required by the IT practitioner in carrying out prototyping
- types of tool which can contribute to prototyping are listed and discussed in more detail in Annex A
- other environmental factors which may affect the success of prototyping.

IT application development managers and project managers must consider these factors carefully before any decision is made on whether, and what, to prototype.

2.3 Management of prototyping

Chapter 5 covers the management of prototyping from estimating and planning through construction, demonstration and review. The chapter defines the project roles specific to prototyping and outlines the key documentation.

2.4 SSADM and prototyping

Chapter 6 shows how various types of prototyping can be fitted into the SSADM modules and how prototyping contributes to SSADM products. Physical Design module (see Figure 1) prototyping is not covered specifically by this volume as it often produces non-throw away code. This type of prototyping will be covered in a further volume.

It is assumed, particularly in Chapter 6, that the reader is familiar with the concepts and terminology of SSADM. For further information, refer to the *SSADM Reference Manuals*.

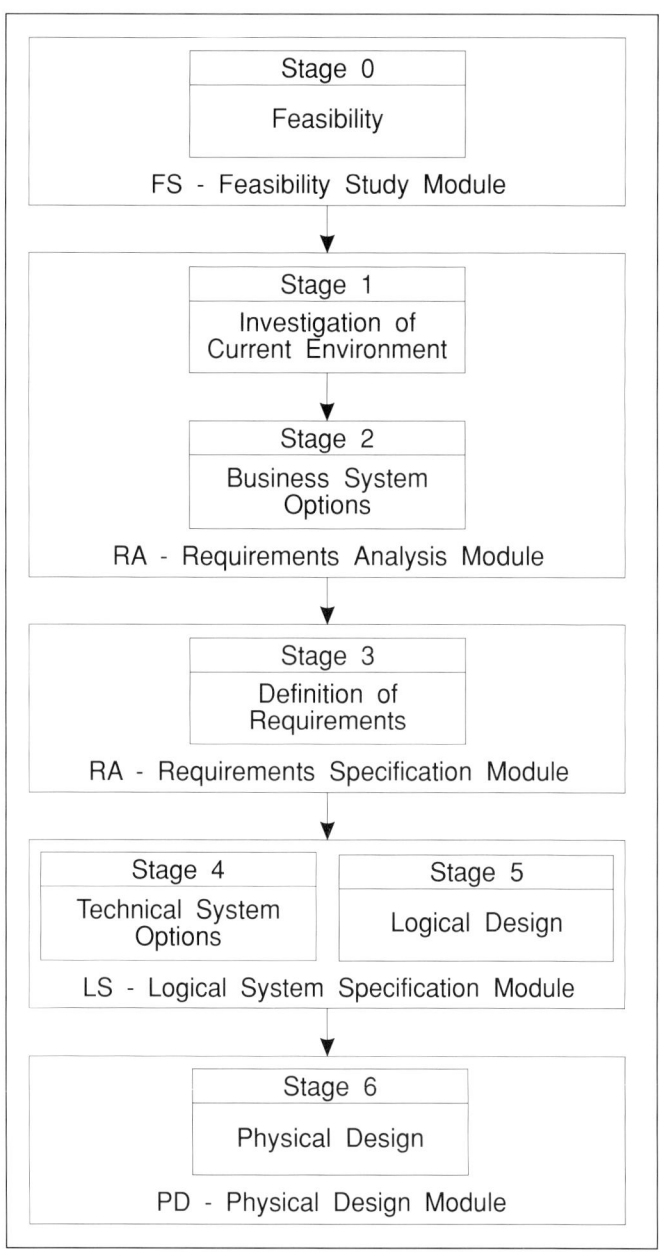

Figure 1: SSADM Modules and Stages

3 Introduction to prototyping

3.1 What is meant by prototyping?

Prototyping has been defined as:

the development of a preliminary version of part or all of a software system to allow certain aspects of that system to be investigated.

Often the primary purpose of a prototype is to obtain feedback from the intended users of the final implementation. The requirements specification for the system can then be updated to reflect this feedback and so increase confidence in the final system. A prototype can be used to investigate particular problem areas or implications of alternative design or implementation decisions.

Prototyping usually involves the users and others to whom the prototype may be shown. Occasionally, it may involve only developers.

Prototyping is an engineering concept whereby a model is produced to check if the design works before being mass produced. The prototype may be costly to build, but it is cheaper than tooling up to build a complete system which does not fulfil the desired needs.

The following types of prototyping are identified and described in this volume:

- Demonstration
- Requirements
- Specification
- Research.

It should be noted that the types of prototyping are subjective and do not have to be followed rigidly. The types are identified to encourage the practitioner to be clear about the objectives of the prototyping and to assist in planning the appropriate activities. In practice there may be hybrids between the types of prototyping covered. For example, there may be a need for a prototype that involves some requirements elicitation to be used as a specification prototype also. The use of such hybrids is acceptable, providing there is a clear view of why the hybrid is necessary and that the objectives can be accomplished.

Demonstration Prototyping

This type of prototyping is intended to facilitate communication between users and developers. The objective is to use the prototype as a demonstration vehicle for particular aspects of a proposed system. The nature of the prototyping process is that the prototype is demonstrated to users or managers and feedback is elicited, but the prototype is not evolved to incorporate that feedback. It is a one-off process and not an iterative one.

Requirements Prototyping

The primary objective of Requirements Prototyping is to improve the quality of the system requirements by:

- clarifying requirements that are not yet clear to the developer
- eliciting further requirements, such as adding more depth to broad initial requirements.

The nature of Requirements Prototyping is that interactive sessions are held between the developer and the user, with the aim of getting the requirements clear by exploring alternatives and stimulating discussion.

Specification Prototyping

The primary objectives of Specification Prototyping are to:

- prove the validity and workability of the specification as a whole or in parts

Chapter 3
Introduction to prototyping

- give the participating users a clearer picture of what the specification means and therefore a better opportunity to influence the way the system is specified
- identify errors in the analysis so far
- enhance the specification.

Research Prototyping

A Research Prototype is normally produced to assist investigation of a complex or difficult area to:

- demonstrate that a particular approach works
- compare results between different approaches.

Research Prototyping may be used at many different points in the SSADM life cycle. It may produce an output that is possible to integrate back into SSADM products, although the type and extent of the output vary enormously.

Chapter 6 covers where the types of prototyping may be used in the SSADM modules.

Certain types of prototyping are not covered in this volume. They are:

- *Implementation prototyping* which is the gradual development of a prototype into the production system. Implementable, rapid application development and incremental are all terms used to describe this approach
- *Prototyping using packages* - when implementing an applications package, it may be possible to prototype using the package as a basis. This is not explicitly covered in the volume, though it may be related to Requirements Prototyping.

3.2 **Why use prototyping?**

There are a number of reasons why prototyping should be considered for use in a system development. The main reasons are given below. For any particular project, the SSADM practitioner can consider those potential benefits which are applicable and use these to determine the case for prototyping at an early stage, for example, in the Feasibility Study module. Figure 2 details the benefits and risks of prototyping.

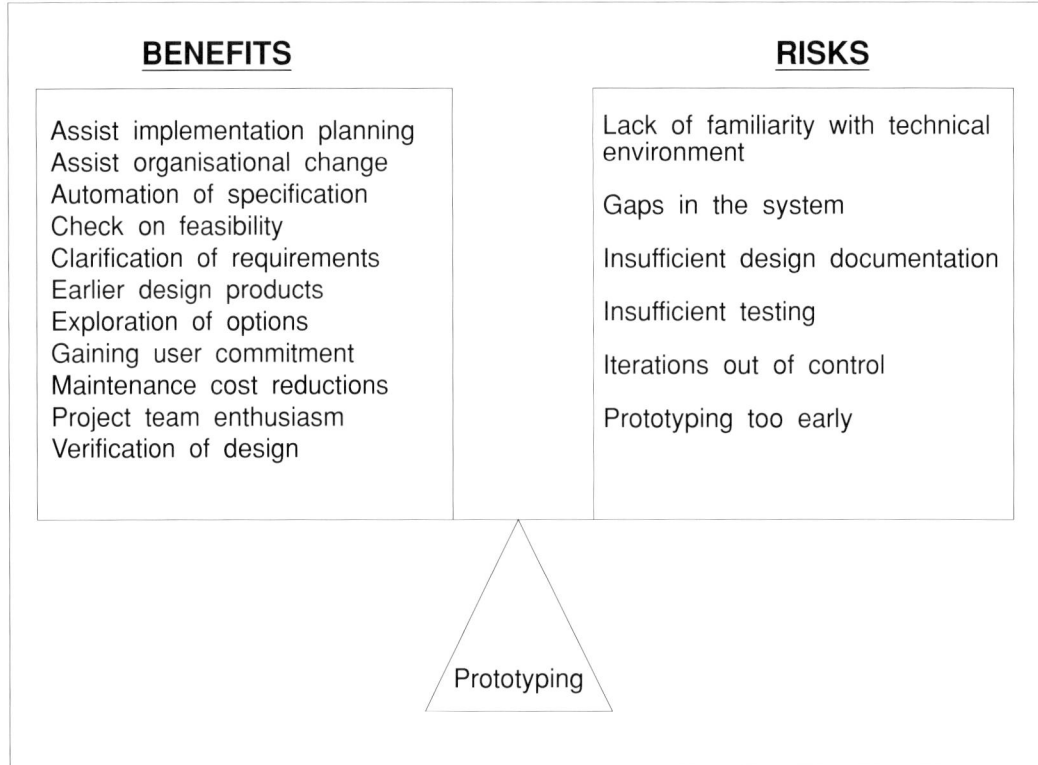

Figure 2: Benefits and risks of prototyping

3.2.1 Clarification of requirements

Prototyping usually increases the chances of the system meeting user requirements. This is because the users participating in the prototyping sessions are able to visualise how the system interfaces with them and will be clearer in defining their requirements.

The requirements being sought may be at the macro level, for example, will this type of approach work?, or at a more detailed level, is this what you want the screen to look like?

The quality of the communication between developers and users is heightened by involvement in the prototyping activity. However, the user must be someone who has the authority to make decisions on what the system needs to do and can approve the results.

3.2.2	Gaining user commitment	The high level of user involvement within projects that use any type of prototyping produces a major benefit. The users take on the ownership of the system being developed because they are helping to build it. They champion the system in the area where it is installed and the system is accepted more readily. This places a higher resource burden on the organisation than normal analysis and design.
3.2.3	Assist organisational change	A prototype can be used to explain the changes implied by a new system or high degree of organisational change. It may enable staff to understand how a new system can fit into the changed organisation and what the changed user roles mean.
3.2.4	Assist implementation planning	By using prototyping, the developer is demonstrating how the system may work in the user environment. This can be of great use when planning the implementation of the system.
3.2.5	Project team enthusiasm	Prototyping improves the enthusiasm of the project team, because the prototyping process produces a result within a reasonable timescale. The project team feel that they are making progress by delivering products and that this is appreciated by the users.
3.2.6	Automation of specification	A prototype is an automated version of part of a specification. It is likely to produce a better, validated specification, which is much better appreciated by the users and has been considered by and demonstrated to the users in a near to real environment.

3.2.7	Verification of designs	A prototype is often a good means of checking that the design meets the requirements. For maximum cost-effectiveness, it may be focused on a specific part of the design, such as a complex process or the data accessing, rather than the entire requirement.
3.2.8	Check for feasibility	A prototype can be built to check the feasibility of a particular approach. For example, it may be used to verify whether a particular process can be automated.
3.2.9	Exploration of options	Prototyping, particularly Requirements Prototyping, gives a chance to explore options with more thoroughness. It provides an opportunity to produce a more effective and higher quality result. It can prevent, for example, the delivery of over-complicated systems due to the development team misconstruing users requirements.
3.2.10	Earlier design products	Prototyping can generate design products at an earlier stage in the analysis and design process. The products may not be in their final form, but they can provide a good start point for the design process. This would apply, for example, to screen formats and dialogue designs.
3.2.11	Specification quality	Prototyping, particularly Specification Prototyping, improves the quality and depth of specifications because of the discipline of building a formal model which has to work. It can, for example, prevent points of detail from being overlooked.
3.2.12	Impact on later SSADM modules	Prototyping in one module usually enables later modules to proceed on a firmer basis. For example, if Requirements Prototyping is carried out in Requirements Analysis, the subsequent Requirements Specification module has a firmer base of documented requirements on which to build.
3.2.13	Maintenance cost reduction	Prototyping can reduce subsequent maintenance costs of the system because a certain amount of testing and validation takes place in the prototyping process. The approach can be used to identify errors that may not otherwise be discovered until the system becomes operational.

Requirements changes, which are a major source of maintenance cost, will be lessened as some will be discovered during the prototyping process and so the extra cost of implementation followed by later change will be avoided.

3.3 Risks of prototyping

Good management of the prototyping process is required to reduce or eliminate some of the problems caused by prototyping. The risks, together with suitable countermeasures, are outlined below.

3.3.1 Prototyping too early

Prototyping before sufficient analysis has been done is a common fault with many prototyping approaches. This volume (Chapter 6) suggests prototyping approaches and where they should be used in the analysis and design process hence overcoming this problem.

3.3.2 Insufficient testing

Insufficiently tested prototypes can lose credibility with the user. Before prototyping sessions are conducted, ensure that testing is carried out with representative data and that obvious failures are rectified.

3.3.3 Unrealistic user expectations

User expectations, such as of delivery timescales, can be raised too high by what appears to be a working system. The participating users should be educated in the process of prototyping and how it fits into the development process.

Users should have a constant reminder of the status of the prototype system being reviewed. This can be achieved, for example, by the word `Prototype' appearing on the screen.

3.3.4 Gaps in the system

Insufficient attention is sometimes paid to aspects of the system which have not been prototyped, such as security, recovery, performance.

The emphasis in this volume is on bringing the results of prototyping back to the normal development process. This gives an opportunity to consolidate specifications and designs and to consider the various aspects left out of the prototype.

3.3.5	Iterations out of control	There is a potential danger that iterations of the prototype review/revise cycle can get out of hand.
		The Project Management section of this volume gives advice on how to control the prototyping process.
3.3.6	Familiarisation with technical environment	Prototyping can become misdirected because of the developers' need to become familiar with a different technical environment - that is, one specific to the prototyping process.
		There is a responsibility on the team leader/project manager to evaluate the technical demands of prototyping before the process starts and to make sure that adequate training and familiarisation in the approach have been allowed.
3.3.7	Insufficient design documentation	Sometimes insufficient design documentation is produced for maintenance purposes. Normally this is due to over reliance on the output of the development tools, including prototyping tools. This volume emphasises the need to produce the relevant SSADM products which should alleviate the problem.
3.4	**When to use prototyping within SSADM**	The developer must decide whether prototyping is feasible for a particular development project. If so, the most relevant type must be selected.

The following checklist indicates the general factors that are conducive to prototyping:

- requirements are known overall but not in detail. If requirements are uncertain, there may not be enough basis for prototyping. If Specification Prototyping is to be undertaken, the requirements must have been established and incorporated in the relevant SSADM products, for example, Logical Data Model (LDM) and Function Definitions. If Requirements Prototyping is to be undertaken, only overall requirements and business objectives need to have been established

- the benefits outweigh the risks (summarised in sections 3.2 and 3.3)
- the type of application to be developed is amenable to prototyping. In general, the on-line parts of systems are more suitable for prototyping
- the risks of not prototyping are too high, for example, the risk of using an uncertain specification is substantial
- the system to be developed is a substantial undertaking with a significant cost of development and implementation, and the cost of prototyping in relation is a low proportion of the overall cost
- the right users are available to participate (Chapters 4 and 5)
- the appropriate skills are available amongst IT developers (Chapter 4)
- the right tools and technical environment are in place (Chapter 4).

If any of the above criteria are not met, any decision to prototype is questionable and must be carefully justified.

A further decision is what type of prototyping to employ. This depends mainly on two key related factors:

- what are the objectives of prototyping for this project?
- what benefits are expected to be achieved from the prototyping exercise?

4 Environmental factors

This chapter gives guidance on the environmental factors which may affect the success of prototyping and on the advantages of the various toolsets which may be used in the process. *Environmental* is used in its broadest sense to include the whole business environment.

Successful prototyping is not confined to very advanced hardware and software environments. The objective of this chapter is to identify which types of tools and other factors are advantageous to the process (see Figure 3). The environmental requirements vary depending on the type of prototyping being carried out.

4.1 User commitment

Greater user commitment to the development process is required when prototyping is used and resource usage is higher compared with other approaches.

The level of activity required varies depending on the type of prototyping being carried out. At the lower end of the scale, not much extra activity is required for Demonstration Prototyping. At the higher end, Specification Prototyping demands a high level of user resource.

Prototyping in an SSADM Environment

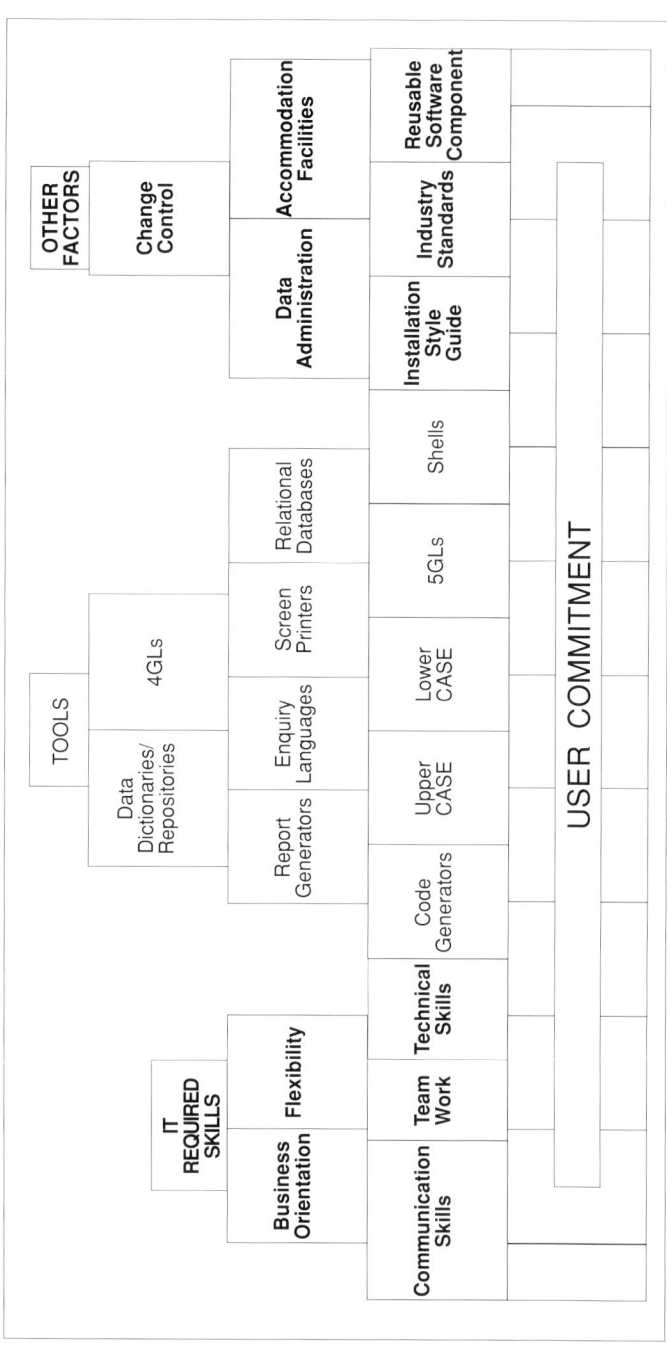

Figure 3: Prototyping environmental factors

The nature of the user commitment can be broken down into a number of separate activities. These are listed in Table 1 and referenced to the types of prototyping.

Type of prototyping User activity	Demon-stration	Require-ments	Specifi-cation	Research
Input to prototype build (e.g. preliminary screens)		√		√
Training/familiarity			√	
Attend sessions	√ (1)	√	√	√ (1)
Evaluation, including recording of comments		√	√	
Review changes to prototype			√	
Review documentation			√	
Sign off/agree	√	√	√	√

(1) = Only one session is likely to be required

Table 1: Type of Prototyping

If the box is not ticked, the involvement is not expected to be very demanding of the user. It does not, however, indicate that there is no involvement.

The actual effort involved in each of these activities varies depending on how much is being prototyped and in which SSADM module. For example, a Demonstration of User Dialogues in Logical System Specification (LSS) is more involved and detailed than a Demonstration related to an Option at Feasibility Study level.

Continuity of user involvement can often make a difference to the success of prototyping. This is particularly true when prototyping is taking place in Requirements Specification (RS) and LSS, due to the level of detail. It is best to ensure that user's time is fully dedicated to the task when they are reviewing such prototypes. As a guide, this could mean that up to three days of dedicated time is required for a prototype of six dialogues and 10 to 20 screens, for example.

Which specific users are invited to participate in the prototyping sessions depends on the objectives of the prototype. For example, the purpose of the prototype may be to determine or confirm fundamental concepts, such as whether certain dialogues are required. In this case, the participating user needs to have sufficient organisational power to be able to take such fundamental decisions on what is presented in the prototype. A different type of user may be required if the objective is to agree the detailed contents of screens or detailed processing aspects.

It is important that both developers and users recognise and accept the degree of involvement required and that it is properly planned from the outset.

4.2 IT required skills

Prototyping demands different and, to some extent, enhanced skills from SSADM practitioners. To a large extent, this can be discerned from the description of the various prototyping methods in Chapter 6. These skills may be provided by a single person or by a team depending on the resource available. Some of the more important considerations are discussed below.

Business orientation

SSADM practitioners in Feasibility Studies, Requirements Analysis (RA) and RS should understand the business of the organisation they are supporting. They should be able to translate the stated business requirements into a prototype that supports those requirements.

Flexibility	The SSADM practitioners involved in the prototyping process must be flexible in their approach to the development. The process is likely to engender a change in the way requirements are translated to dialogues, screens and other system products.
Communication skills	Prototyping demands and uses a high degree of communication both between participating users and developers and within prototyping teams. The developer has to explain the technical implications of meeting requirements to the user, so that sensible decisions can be agreed. The developer also has to understand the users description of the functions/services required.
	The effectiveness of prototyping is seriously downgraded if communication skills are deficient. This applies to all forms of prototyping but is more important for Requirements and Specification Prototyping.
Teamwork	Prototyping works best with small, skilled and tightly-knit teams. Developers must be capable of working in such an environment as opposed to a large structure.
Technical skills	The building and subsequent revision of prototypes is often under considerable time pressure. This puts a premium on the technical ability of developers to produce workable prototypes quickly.
	Normally, a production tool of some type is required to develop prototypes, such as for quick building of screens and dialogues. Often it is supported by a data dictionary. The developer needs to have the skill in using these tools to advantage.
	The process requires rapid adjustments to be made to the prototype, particularly in Requirements Prototyping. These are not normally made in the user's presence (see section 5.5.4 Workshops) but need to be turned round in a timescale of days rather than weeks, if the process is not to lose momentum. Typically, the Requirements Prototype requires proficiency in at least some of the following system build components:

- screen construction

- dialogue construction
- screen item definition, editing and validation
- menu structure definition
- user interface mechanics such as dialogue boxes, options, messages etc
- process logic definition such as basic processing via a Fourth Generation Language (4GL)
- data dictionary/repository.

Similar pressures apply in Specification Prototyping but the prototype is likely to embody more of the system at a greater depth than the Requirements Prototype. For example, it may include some data accessing, which adds a layer of complexity to the model. This implies a similar skill set to those listed above, but generally with a higher degree of 4GL skill and possibly database/file design as well.

4.3 Tools

Before undertaking any type of prototyping, a decision must be made on the technical environment to be used, including the set of development tools for prototyping. This volume gives general guidance on the criteria to use for selection of certain types of tool. It does not name or recommend specific tools.

In Annex A, details are given for each major tool type that may be used for prototyping, these are:

- Data Dictionaries/Repositories
- 4GLs
- Relational Databases
- Screen Painters
- Enquiry Languages
- Report Generators
- Code Generators
- Upper Computer Aided Software Engineering (CASE) Tools

- Lower CASE Tools
- Fifth Generation Languages (5GLs) and Extensions
- Shells such as expert system shells, object shells.

The information given for each tool includes:

- definition and essential characteristics
- its overall contribution to prototyping
- generic features to look for which are useful to prototyping.

4.4 Other environmental factors

Further environmental factors that may affect the success of prototyping are outlined below.

4.4.1 Accommodation facilities

Prototyping requires that the developer(s) and user(s) are able to review the prototype together. For this purpose, a large enough area with suitable terminals or personal computers (PCs) should be set aside. It is useful to have a printing facility, for example, to produce hard copies of the information displayed on screens. In addition, there needs to be facilities for writing down comments and possibly a white board for drawing diagrams etc. There should be an easy means of recording such material, such as a camera or photocopyable white board.

As well as being accessible at the time the prototype is being reviewed, it may be useful in some cases to allow users access to review the prototype on an ad hoc basis. It is important that the environment is as free as possible from outside interruptions during prototype reviews.

Demonstration prototyping usually takes place either formally in a meeting room, or informally in the normal user or development environment.

4.4.2 Installation style guide

The Installation Style Guide contains the installation standards that apply to various features of the development, including:

- human computer interface
- screen formats
- report styles
- dialogues such as navigation features, style of help screens
- data naming, validation.

The existence of comprehensive standards in these areas greatly improves the effectiveness of prototyping, enabling it to concentrate on essential functionality.

It may be necessary to compromise between standards and tool capability. These compromises must be documented and agreement sought for acceptance.

4.4.3 Data administration

The prototyping activities may need to interface with the data administration function. This is particularly true if multiple prototypes are being developed within the same project, for example, for different business areas. The changes made to data definitions must be coordinated and ultimately subjected to the installation's data disciplines. Whether this happens during the prototyping process or in a consolidation activity after prototyping is complete, is a project management issue and depends on the type of prototyping and the degree of change.

4.4.4 Change control

Prototyping often involves frequent changes to the system objects being prototyped and therefore needs a system of change control that can cope with rapid change. See the ITIL Guide on Change Management. The change control system should include the following features:

- version control for all development objects such as programs, screens, etc
- identification of configuration of each prototype version
- status identification of each requested change.

Without such a system, there is a danger that the volume of changes will cause the prototype development to get out of control.

There is less requirement for such facilities for a simple Demonstration or Requirements Prototype. There is generally a greater need for formalised change control when a number of iterations of reviewing and revising the prototype are planned.

4.4.5 Reusable software components

If a library of software components has been built up, prepared application skeletons and so on, these can be used to speed up the process of prototype construction. The components may be from related projects, or existing installed systems. The effectiveness of such an approach depends on being able to identify the right components. This depends on their having been adequately documented.

As with the use of Shells, the approach may constrain the type and nature of the prototype which can be built.

5 Management of prototyping

This chapter gives guidance on how the prototyping aspects of SSADM projects should be managed.

The following aspects of project management are considered:

- project organisation, with particular focus on the prototyping teams and participants
- estimating of prototyping activities
- producing the Prototyping Plan
- negotiation with users
- managing prototyping sessions
- evaluation of feedback from users on the prototype
- control of the prototyping cycle
- documentation standards for prototypes.

5.1 Project staffing

The staffing of a project needs to take account of the fact that prototyping is taking place. The type of prototyping taking place may or may not make a difference to the staffing of the project. For example, producing a demonstration prototype in Feasibility Study is unlikely to change the staffing required. Conversely, producing a Specification Prototype in Requirements Specification requires specific roles to be defined, for example, user representatives at the prototyping sessions.

The roles which need to be defined or expanded in connection with prototyping are:

- User Representative
- Prototyping Team Leader
- Team Member
- Change Manager.

Prototyping in an SSADM Environment

See Figure 4 for an explanation of suggested relationships between these roles.

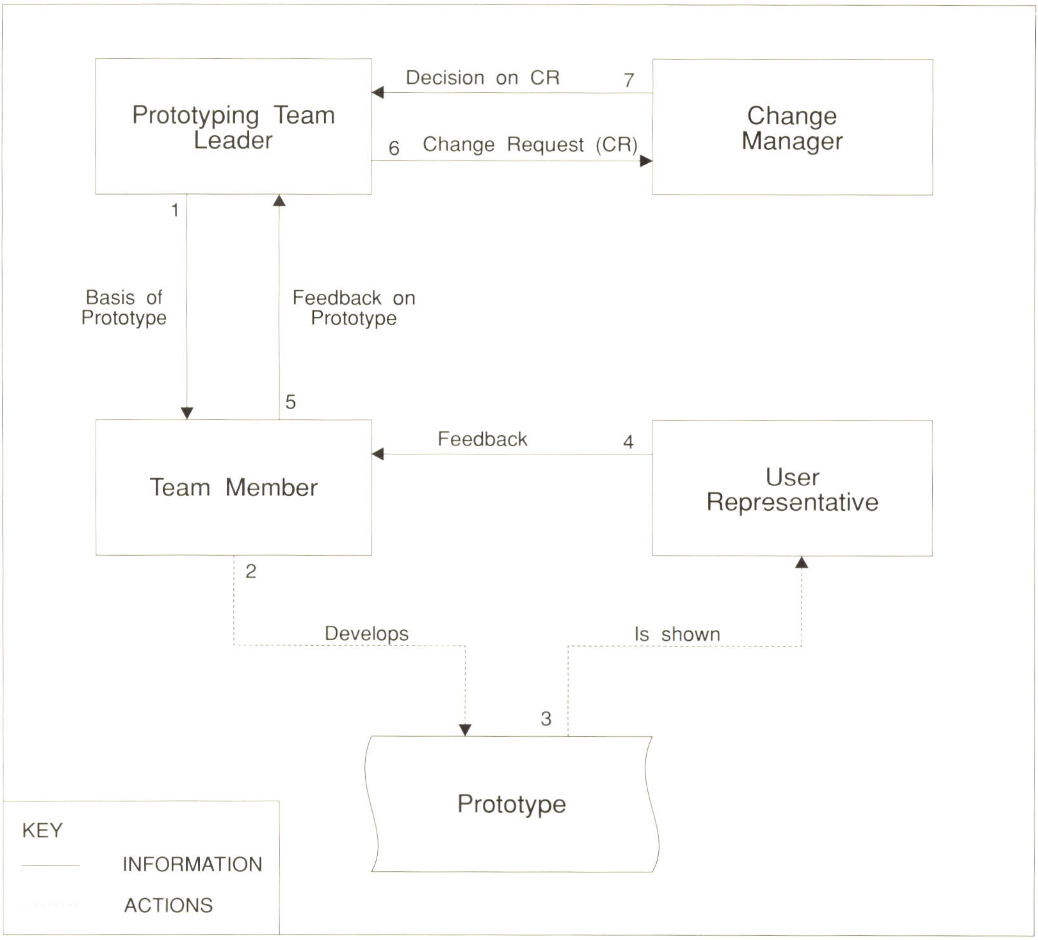

```
                        Decision on CR        7
    Prototyping Team  ◄──────────────────  Change
         Leader        ──────────────────► Manager
                     6  Change Request (CR)
         │ ▲
       1 │ │
         │ │
    Basis of  Feedback on
   Prototype   Prototype
         │ │ 5
         ▼ │                Feedback       4
    Team Member  ◄────────────────────── User Representative
              │                                    ▲
            2 │                                    │
              │    Develops          Is shown      │
              └──────────────┐  ┌─────────────────┘
                             ▼  │
                              3
                           Prototype

   KEY
   ─────── INFORMATION
   ------- ACTIONS
```

Figure 4:   Main Roles and Functions within Prototyping (General)

User Representative in prototyping sessions — This role is vital and central to all but Research Prototyping. The number of users to be actively invoived must be balanced against the volume of reviewing to be done, the development support that can be given, the timescales of the stage or module, the availability and suitability of users.

The essential characteristics which user(s) in this role must have are outlined below:

- appropriate level of knowledge of the business aspects being prototyped, which could range from high level knowledge of business function requirements to lower level knowledge of the processing or data details

- appropriate level of authority to take or, at least, recommend decisions

- ability to communicate with the prototyping team

- representative of the user community. The representation must take account of a number of factors including:

    - experience of computer systems. If only experienced users are chosen, they may take decisions which are not commensurate with the ability of the rest of the community

    - geographical location. It is good practice to take a cross-section of users at different sites when a number of sites are involved

    - experience of business processes and business goals. If only user managers are chosen, the actual processes that the user undertakes may not be fully reflected. However there must be an understanding among the user representatives of the business goals if not a very short term solution may be developed

    - business areas that the system covers. If the new system and the prototype embrace operational and management information aspects, then the two groups must be represented.

Prototyping team leader

The prototyping Team Leader is responsible for:

- deciding which functions and user roles are to be prototyped using the Prototyping Scope as a basis (see section 5.3 Prototype planning)

- management of the prototyping development effort from initial build to any subsequent revisions, for example, ensuring that adequate testing is carried out. This includes determining timescale for successful completion and also the resources required to undertake the task

- deciding who is to participate in the prototyping sessions

- evaluation of user feedback from the prototyping sessions, and proposal of necessary changes

- control of the iterations of the prototyping cycle, within the constraints of the project plan, that is, deciding whether a further iteration is necessary

- producing the Prototyping Report, which summarises the results of the prototyping sessions and how far objectives have been met.

It is vital that strong team leadership is employed, to ensure that the iterative prototyping process does not get out of control. The Team Leader is also responsible for the quality assurance/quality inspection of the prototype. It is also vital that the Team Leader has analytical skills and an awareness of the prototyping tools. The detailed expertise in the use and application of the tool is supplied by members of the project team.

For a demonstration prototype, the role of Team Leader should still be present but the degree of management required is much less.

Team member	The Team Members need to be able to build and change the prototype quickly. For this reason, they need to be skilled in the use of the selected tool. In addition, as they are going to be identifying the requirements and specifications with the users, they will need analytical skills and a high degree of communication skills. See section 4.2 IT Required skills, Technical skills.
Change manager	The Change Manager role may be carried out in practice by the prototyping Team Leader. This section indicates the specific responsibilities for change management, which are:

- ensuring that all user requests are documented, categorised and translated into changes where necessary
- ensuring that all requested changes are assessed and actioned. These may be implemented or a decision made not to implement
- assessment of the impact of changes on the progress of the prototype.

5.2 Estimating

Estimating the prototyping activities is essential to produce a meaningful Prototyping Plan. Estimating is made more problematic by the fact that prototyping can be an iterative process. The following estimating approaches may be used for prototyping:

- bottom-up
- by analogy
- constraint models
- product based
- contingency
- use of metrics.

See Annex B for further details.

5.3 Prototype planning

A Prototyping Plan must be produced for any form of prototyping. Note that the Prototyping Plan is an expansion of what is contained in the Stage plan and must be consistent with it. The suggested contents of the plan are:

- *Prototyping Scope*

    This defines the functions and user roles which are to be prototyped, the resources to be employed and the constraints which apply. It is produced before the prototyping activity commences and is an overall narrative which is expanded by the remainder of the plan.

- *Objectives of the Prototype*

    This defines the objectives and the type of prototype to be employed.

- *Product Breakdown Structure and allied documentation*

    The structure indicates the products which are to be produced as a result of prototyping. They must be documented as Product Descriptions.

- *Environment Requirements*

    An outline of the computer system and tools requirements for the prototyping activity.

- *Activity Plan*

    This shows the activity breakdown for the prototyping activity with durations, effort and allocated staff. It is normally produced as a bar chart.

- *Resource Plan*

    This shows the usage and costs of all resources, including developer and user time, for the prototyping activity.

Chapter 5
Management of prototyping

- *Project Organisation*

    The prototyping team, user representatives, team management, links to IT and user management and to the remainder of the development project are all defined.

- *Quality Plan*

    The quality criteria for the prototype, defining fitness for purpose and how this may be assessed.

- *Documentation*

    The prototype must be properly documented to record the results. SSADM prototyping documentation, as shown in the *SSADM Reference Manual*, should be produced.

5.4 Negotiation

Negotiation is always an element of the system development process. Where prototyping is being used, it becomes more prominent. Users have the opportunity to influence the system produced, by making requests during prototype review. There are a number of dangers in the process, for example:

- unrealistic requests may be put forward by the users and accepted by the developers because:
    - developers are not fully aware of the priority of the request to the business and the business benefit it would bring
    - users may not be aware of the development implications and the cost of their request
- developers and users may spend too much time looking at cosmetic and presentational features, rather than at the functionality of the system
- users and developers spend too long exploring trivial issues
- developers produce a system not appropriate for the user's business.

The purpose of negotiation is to avoid these and other pitfalls. There are a number of negotiating principles which should be borne in mind by both sides, which help to avoid these dangers. The main ones are as follows:

- ensure that a list of the issues and objectives which relate to a prototyping session is prepared. Note the minimum position which the developer or team are prepared to accept for each one without jeopardising their objectives. This may be documented as part of the Prototype Demonstration Objective Document

- when discussing issues with the other parties, ask questions to determine their true needs. Always discuss alternatives and continue, if possible, until a mutually satisfactory conclusion is reached

- summarise the position reached in a discussion to ensure that it is clearly understood and accepted by both sides

- not to reach formal agreement without gaining all the necessary information. It is not necessary to settle every issue in a session as some issues may take further work and reflection before being satisfactorily resolved.

5.5 Managing prototyping sessions

Prototyping sessions, that is, reviews of the prototype with users, are at the core of the prototyping approach, and must be properly managed. The sessions vary in character depending on the type of prototype, its extent, the numbers of people involved and the stage the project has reached. There are nevertheless overall principles as well as specific issues which are outlined below.

5.5.1 Definition of a session

In all cases, it is necessary to be firm about the scope of the prototype which is the subject of the session. If the overall prototype scope is likely to make the session too long or otherwise unmanageable, it must be divided up and separate sessions held. The Prototyping Results Log is used to record the findings of all sessions.

Demonstration prototyping	In this case, the session is concerned more with communication and less with interaction. The onus is on the development team to provide a concise and effective demonstration. Demonstrations should be as short as possible, anything over one hour is likely to prove unsuccessful. The number of users involved may be larger than for interactive sessions.
	The session should conclude with questions from the attendees and should produce an agreed list of points and issues.
Requirements prototyping	In these sessions, the emphasis is on interaction to drive out the requirements. The initial prototype provides a start point from which more information and changes to the prototype are built up. The sessions may be longer than for Demonstration Prototyping, for example, up to half a day. The number of users should be limited to those who can effectively contribute in the sessions. Typically, this is two or three at most.
	The actual manipulation of the prototype during Requirements Prototyping is controlled by the developer, but may include hands-on time for the user. Simple changes may be made to the prototype during the course of the sessions provided that the tool facilitates this. Care must be taken not to spend too much effort on changes during sessions. Too much time spent on modifications can demotivate the user, whose objective is to see the system not to watch the developer manipulating programs. Changes should only be undertaken where they may make a real difference to the user's perception of the system. However, if a cosmetic change makes the user more comfortable with the prototype, then it should be made.
	Requirements Prototyping is normally expected to be less formal than either Demonstration or Specification Prototyping. This does not take away the need to properly document the outcome.

	Specification prototyping	This is expected to be a more formal session than a requirements session. The characteristic of this type of prototyping is the level of detail which may be addressed. There will be interaction in the sessions and there is some scope for exploring possibilities. However, the initial prototype is expected to be close to the required result and the adjustments are mostly minor. The Specification Prototype sessions may be repeated two or three times with requested changes implemented in between the sessions. Some consideration should be given as to whether it is necessary to review the whole prototype at each successive session, or whether a portion can be signed off and the scope reduced for the next session. If the scope is large, a number of sessions within the same cycle may be held to cover different aspects of the prototype.
	Research prototyping	This usually requires only informal sessions whilst the prototype is being developed. On completion, it may be useful to hold a demonstration session so that all relevant parties are made aware of the results of the prototype.
5.5.2	Roles of participants	There should always be at least one developer and one user at a prototyping session. The overall roles are as follows:

- Developer
  - explains the concept of the prototype to the user
  - demonstrates the prototype
  - answers user queries
  - logs user responses and requests
  - ensures all key issues and objectives are addressed
  - negotiates with the user
  - reports back to the Team Leader

- User

    - observes the prototype and may sometimes do hands-on exercising of the prototype

    - raises comments and questions on the prototype

    - may take decisions on requirements or design preferences, depending on the level of authority

    - refers issues to other users, as appropriate, possibly after the session

    - negotiates with the developer.

For larger sessions, it may be necessary to have further roles. For example, the Team Leader may chair the session to ensure that objectives are met if a larger group of developers and users is involved. A further useful addition for larger sessions may be a secretary to take notes, ensure that logs are filled in, etc. The latter role is more likely to be effective in a demonstration session than in an interactive one.

In general, the maximum size for a formal interactive session should be two developers and two to three users.

5.5.3 Supporting material

The prototyping session is largely focused on the computer system being demonstrated. It is essential to have a minimum amount of supporting material to assist the process. The following items are suggested:

- explanation of objectives, which only needs the key points to be written on a sheet of paper or a flip chart

- help material on using the prototype, particularly if the users are expected to do some hands-on exercising of the prototype

- forms on which users may write comments, these could be pre-printed with the date, project/session identifier and topic headings

- Prototype Result Log, on which the developer records results including required changes.

In addition, it is often useful to be able to print copies of screens in the sessions which can then be annotated in order to clarify particular points.

5.5.4 Workshops

The principle of a workshop may be utilised to enhance the value which can be gained from prototyping sessions. This involves increasing the involvement and activity of the user role. It is particularly valuable to do this in Requirements Prototypes where there is a degree of uncertainty in the requirements detail.

A workshop is a formal meeting whose objective is to resolve issues by debate, with all sides stating their views and eventually coming to an agreement. Some of the main reasons for adopting a workshop approach are summarised as follows:

- there are at least three contributors
- there are different points of view
- the users are geographically widespread
- the scope of the prototype is large but is difficult to break into separate sessions
- the proposed system is a radical departure from current practice and there is a need to get broad consensus on the future direction.

A workshop needs to be managed by a facilitator, whose role is to ensure that the workshop meets its objectives.

Joint Application Design (JAD) is a further development of the workshop approach. It involves leading the users through the whole analysis and design process within a workshop. It may involve prototyping along the way but is much wider in scope than prototyping. It is not covered in any detail in this volume.

5.6 Evaluation of user feedback

The prototyping process must deal with a number of aspects concerned with obtaining and analysing feedback from users. The type of feedback which can be expected varies according to the type of prototyping being undertaken and is covered below according to type.

5.6.1 Demonstration prototyping

Feedback is often in the form of unstructured oral comments. To ensure that information is not lost, it is advisable to ensure that one person at the demonstration is available to take notes. A further possibility is to hand out questionnaires that can be filled in by the attendees. This has the merit of organising users' thoughts into a consistent framework. For example, the questionnaire could have sections on Appearance, Functionality etc, with further categories specific to the development.

It is unlikely that feedback from a demonstration will be detailed. The task of the development team after the session is to organise the feedback into consistent headings, and qualify each comment or request according to:

- importance to the user
- impact on the development
- urgency.

Impact would be analysed in the same way as the Prototype Result Log, such as *No Change Required, Cosmetic*, etc.

After a demonstration prototyping session, the results of the feedback analysis should be sent to the participating users. The users should place the comments/requests in order of importance. This gives the users a chance to reflect on the prototype as a whole and may provide a more objective assessment of the results.

5.6.2 Requirements prototyping

As Requirements Prototyping is an interactive process, there is an opportunity for the developer to take careful note of the points being made and to agree these with the user as part of the session. This means that a reasonably well organised and documented set of information should come out of the process.

Prototyping in an SSADM Environment

It is worthwhile producing a feedback sheet in advance of the sessions, which has the main topics as headings. It is suggested that the following areas would normally be covered:

- new functions
- changes to functions
- new User Roles
- changes to User Roles
- changes to menus
- new dialogues
- changes to dialogues
- new screens
- changes to screens
- new data
- changes to data definitions
- new processing
- changes to processing.

Not all comments and requests fall neatly into one category, but may span several. All requests should be recorded in the Requirements Catalogue and given a priority, together with other recorded requirements. It is particularly important that changes expressed at the physical level, such as a change to a prototype screen, are reflected in the logical model as the physical products are not carried forward.

5.6.3 Specification prototyping

This process is similar to that described for Requirements Prototyping. Because Specification Prototyping starts from a more solid base of analysis, it is expected that the feedback will contain more detailed points and less global ones. Depending on how the session is run, it is probably useful to provide users with feedback sheets on which to write their comments under structured headings.

Chapter 5
Management of prototyping

At the end of each session, the comments and requests need to be accepted by the prototyping team. The recommended sequence of events is as follows:

- record all feedback on the Prototyping Result Log, this includes grading each result. Refer to the *SSADM Version 4 Reference Manual* for recommended grading criteria

- assess the work required to build in the changes to the prototype and to any SSADM products

- if required, build the next version of the prototype, this helps to validate the changes

- make any necessary changes to the SSADM products such as the LDM.

5.7 Control of prototyping

Project Management and the Prototyping Team Leader carry responsibility for the success of the prototyping process. The Team Leader is primarily in control of the prototyping aspect and reports to the Module, Stage or Project Manager if there are problems.

The main points of control are indicated in Figure 5.

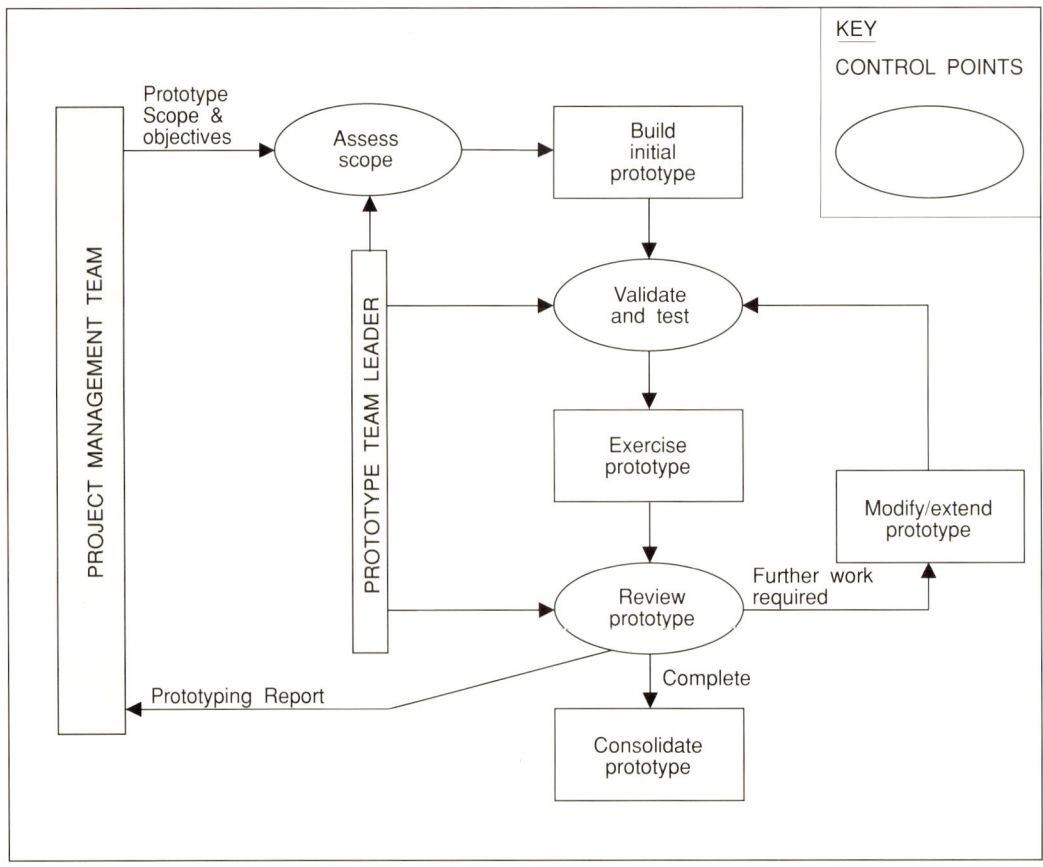

Figure 5: Control of prototyping

As part of assessing the Prototyping Scope, a firm decision must be made to constrain the prototyping activity by one or more of the following:

- the total effort for the prototyping activity, users and developers, possibly just developers can be limited to a set budget. Any increase in the budget can only be approved by project management or possibly the Project Board.

    This would need to be formally requested and justified following the review of the prototype by the prototyping team

Chapter 5
Management of prototyping

- the number of times the prototyping process is repeated (see Figure 5) can be limited, for example, to three iterations. Again, any relaxation of the limit would be on the approval of project management

- a time limit may be set, for example, the prototyping must be completed within two weeks

- a diminishing returns rule may be employed, for example, when the number of changes/comments fall to a certain level, the prototype is regarded as exhausted.

Whatever approach is adopted, it is important that users as well as developers understand the chosen mechanism of control. Users should be given an opportunity to agree that the prototype can be signed off. It is an important control that the users sign off the prototype, at least for Requirements and Specification Prototyping, and record any outstanding reservations they may have.

Project Management is the responsibility of the Project Manager and the Stage Manager. On each iteration of the cycle when the prototype is reviewed, it is essential to review the scope of what is to be built and exercised in the next cycle.

It should be noted that the scope does not exceed that originally envisaged for the prototype and documented in the prototyping plan. If it does, it must be brought to the attention of the Project Manager and authorisation to proceed must be sought

Where the mechanism of control is a number of iterative cycles, the progress of the prototype should be measured. This entails measuring the:

- number of outstanding issues, possibly as a percentage of the number of original issues listed on the Prototype Objectives form

- number of dialogues and screens now agreed, as a percentage of the total

- estimated effort to revise and demonstrate.

5.8 Documentation

At the end of the prototyping activities, it is essential to produce a report, however brief, which summarises the results of the prototyping. The Prototyping Report should be addressed to the Project Manager and possibly Project Board. The latter applies if the prototyping activity requires decisions to be made by the Project Board. Further details about the Prototyping Report can be obtained from the *SSADM Reference Manual*, but there is no predetermined structure defined.

Prototyping Report

The following is a suggested contents list:

Objectives	This may refer to the Prototyping Plan and Prototyping Scope within the plan.
Achievements	Coverage of the objectives and whether they have been met or not and overall user rating of the prototype.
Products	The main SSADM products that have been created or substantially updated as a result of prototyping.
Budget	The effort and timescale versus plan.
Issues	Issues originally expected to be resolved by prototyping that remain unresolved and any new issues emerging, such as changes in the scope of the prototype.
Lessons	Lessons learnt for future prototyping exercises, for example, concerning the environment, the tools used, the approach.

It is not mandatory to produce all these sections. If, for example, a brief demonstration was produced in the Feasibility Study module, the report may be just a few lines explaining the result.

Chapter 6
SSADM and prototyping

6 SSADM and prototyping

This chapter explains the approach that needs to be taken for each type of prototyping. It defines how each approach interfaces with SSADM activities and products. It is organised by SSADM modules and references each type of prototyping. Note that not all types of prototyping are relevant in each module of SSADM.

SSADM Module Type of prototyping	Feasibility Study	Requirements Analysis	Requirements Specification	Logical System Specification
Demonstration	√	√		√
Requirements		√	√	√
Specification			√	√
Research	√			√

Table 2: Types of prototyping and their use in SSADM

For each type of prototyping that is relevant within a module (see Table 2), this chapter:

- gives guidelines on the overall approach

- indicates the inputs into the prototyping process in terms of SSADM products

- indicates the outputs that are produced from prototyping and the SSADM products into which they are incorporated.

6.1 Feasibility Study module

Figure 6 shows suggested types of prototyping for use in the Feasibility Study module.

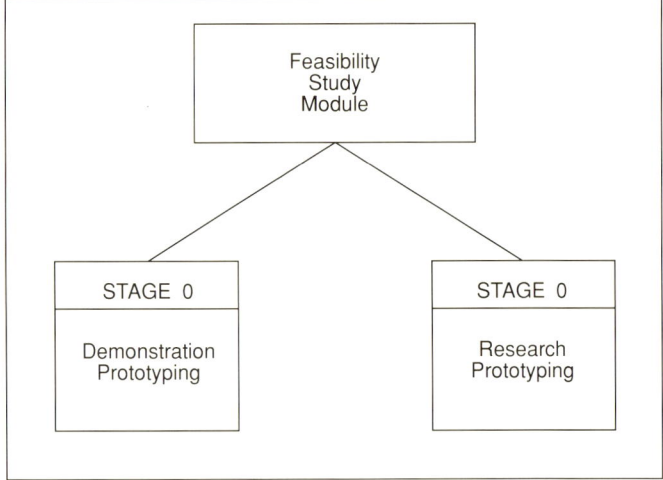

Figure 6: Prototyping types in Feasibility Study module

6.1.1 Demonstration prototyping (FS)

Ideally the need to prototype should be identified at the beginning of the study, so that the appropriate resources can be planned. However, it may be that the need to produce a Demonstration Prototype emerges during the study.

The following points should be considered when producing a Demonstration Prototype at this stage:

- choose the appropriate hardware, software, and supporting tools. This should be geared to rapid production, without necessarily being the target environment, but not so far removed from the target environment as to be unrepresentative. For example, it should have the basic look and feel of the target environment, so far as it is known

Chapter 6
SSADM and prototyping

- be very selective of what needs to be demonstrated, pick only those key aspects where a demonstration is of real value. For example, the purpose of the demonstration may be to show that workstation graphical output can be used in place of paperwork in the existing system. A simple mocked-up example with a small piece of representative data often suffices to model this feature

- test the prototype sufficiently to ensure it is robust enough for the demonstration

- produce a list of issues that the development team is expecting to resolve by demonstrating the prototype and ensure that the demonstration covers these.

Interface with SSADM	The prototype(s) should reflect one or more of the composite options produced as part of Step 030, Select Feasibility Options.
	The fact that a prototype is being produced does not take away the need to produce a proper description of the options.
Products	All decisions and information resulting from the prototype and its demonstration must be recorded as one or more of:

- Option Description(s)
- Requirements in the Requirements Catalogue
- Outline Required Environment Description.

The Feasibility Report is the key SSADM product. All information recorded in the above categories potentially contribute to the Feasibility Report.

6.1.2 Research prototyping (FS)   The use of Research Prototyping in this module must be focused on a specific problem that is central to the Feasibility Study objectives. It must address the technical or business feasibility of a proposed new system.

The following guidelines should be considered when producing a Research Prototype in this module:

- produce a Prototyping Scope, which gives clear terms of reference for the Research Prototype. The scope should be strictly limited to what is required for Feasibility Study purposes. There is a great danger of trying to go too far with a prototype at this early point in the development

- the time required to produce a prototype may significantly lengthen the Feasibility Study timescale. It is important therefore that the relevant plan is reviewed for accuracy and that the impact is agreed by the Project Board

- the prototype is implemented and reviewed once, it is not developed in an iterative way. The review and sign-off authorities for the prototype must be defined in the Prototyping Scope

- carry out the prototyping within a defined timescale and budget, bearing in mind the Feasibility Study constraints

- there are no specific tool guidelines that can be given for this type of prototyping, as there is a variety of possible functions and system aspects that may be prototyped. The potential areas for Research Prototyping include:

    - specific hardware, for example, database management system (DBMS) engines

    - use of DBMS, specific operating systems, etc

    - type of user interface

    - algorithms

    - system interfaces

    - reorganisation of business functions.

Interface with SSADM	The Research Prototype is normally produced for one or more composite options (Business System Option (BSO) and Technical System Option (TSO)) but not until these options have been explored and defined. Exceptionally, it may be relevant as a precondition to all options as it may, for example, be aimed at whether a function can be computerised at all.

The prototype may be revisited when TSOs are reviewed again in the LSS module. |
| Products | The results of the Research Prototype, including the reviewer's assessment, are included in the Feasibility Options. There are a number of headings to which the prototype results may contribute:

- software and hardware configuration required
- impact analysis
- resource requirements of the options
- business or technical risks
- advantages and disadvantages of the options. |

6.2 Requirements Analysis module

Two types of prototyping are potentially relevant here, Demonstration and Requirements. In either case, take care to ensure that the prototype is not developed beyond the point of cost effectiveness. With Requirements Prototyping the requirements identified may not be included in the selected Business System Option (BSO) and time may therefore be wasted.

Prototyping in an SSADM Environment

Figure 7 shows suggested types of prototyping for use in the Requirements Analysis module.

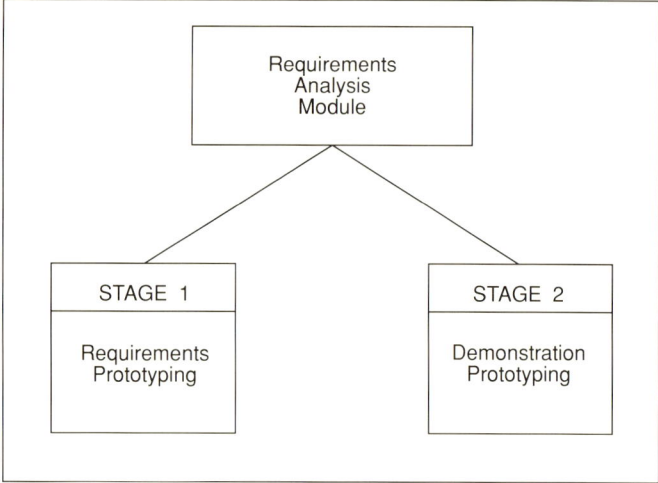

Figure 7: Prototyping types in Requirements Analysis module

6.2.1 Requirements prototyping (RA)

The major use of Requirements Prototyping is in this module with the prime objective of clarifying requirements. New requirements may also be elicited.

The following points should be considered when producing a Requirements Prototype in this module:

- ensure that the requirements have been identified and recorded as comprehensively as possible, before any prototypes are developed and that they are documented in the Requirements Catalogue

- identify the requirements that are unclear, which seem good candidates for prototyping

- consider which users should be involved in the interactive sessions and also which developers should be involved

Chapter 6
SSADM and prototyping

- set a time and effort limit within which the prototyping process must take place. Ensure that the Stage plan covers the necessary activities and effort
- consider whether the Requirements Prototype, or part of it, may be carried forward to help define the BSOs.

Interface with SSADM

Potential input products to prototyping, whether Demonstration or Requirements, in this module are:

- Current system DFDs
- Requirements Catalogue
- User Catalogue.

Requirements Prototyping is carried out as an addition to Step 120, Investigate and Define Requirements, and as such is in parallel with Steps 130 and 140, concerning current processes and data.

Products

The key products are:

- Prototyping Scope which as well as being an input to the prototyping process is also a valuable output when it records the scope of the work actually done
- application products from the prototype itself, typically including screen contents, data used and processing definition in some form
- Prototype Result Log, in this case containing the user reactions to the prototyping sessions in more detail than in Demonstration Prototyping.

Following Requirements Prototyping, information from the activity is incorporated into SSADM products, primarily:

- Requirements Catalogue
- User Catalogue
- Data Catalogue

- BSOs definition prior to selection of the BSO.

6.2.2 Demonstration prototyping (RA)

The following guidelines should be considered when producing a Demonstration Prototype in this module:

- the purpose of the prototype is to show how particular requirements are met by the defined BSOs. With this in mind, decide which BSOs need to be prototyped and which specific functions within the BSOs

- choose the appropriate hardware, software, and supporting tools. This should be geared to rapid production, without necessarily being the target environment, but not so far removed from the target environment as to be unrepresentative

- test the prototype sufficiently to ensure it is robust enough for the demonstration

- consider whether the prototype, or part of it, needs to be used as a demonstration to the Project Board before the formal End-Stage Assessment takes place and make any necessary small adjustments, for example, to make it run smoothly

- produce a list of the issues that the development team is expecting to resolve by demonstrating the prototype and ensure that the demonstration covers these.

Interface with SSADM

Potential input products to prototyping, whether Demonstration or Requirements, in this module are:

- Current system DFDs
- Requirements Catalogue
- User Catalogue
- Prototyping Scope which may be developed as the first step in prototyping.

Demonstration Prototyping is carried out in Step 220, Select Business System Option, but may occasionally be started in Step 210, Define Business System Options.

	Products	The key products are:

- Prototyping Scope, the scope is an input to the prototyping process, however, following prototyping, it is a valuable output to record the actual scope of what was done

- application products from the prototype itself, typically including screen contents, data used and processing definition in some form

- Prototype Result Log, in this case containing brief notes of the reactions to the demonstration.

Following Demonstration Prototyping, information from the activity is incorporated into SSADM products, primarily:

- Requirements Catalogue
- User Catalogue
- Data Catalogue prior to BSOs
- the BSOs definition, if the prototype was demonstrated in this context.

6.3 Requirements Specification module

Figure 8 shows suggested types of prototyping for use in the Requirements Specification module.

Prototyping in an SSADM Environment

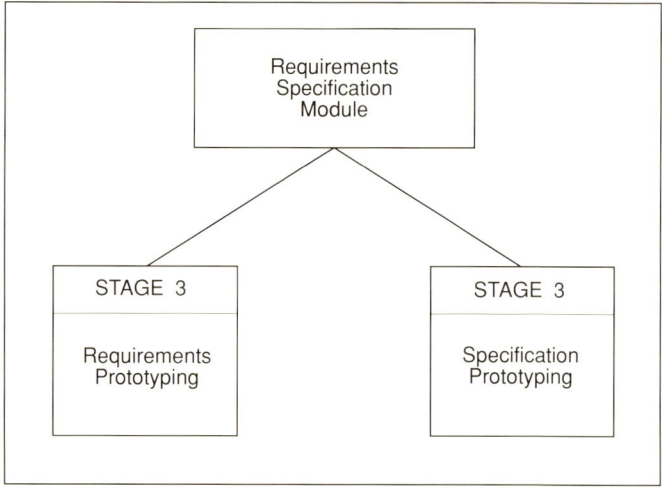

Figure 8: Prototyping types in Requirements Specification module

6.3.1 Requirements Prototyping (RS)

Requirements Prototyping is used at a greater level of detail in this module, with the objective of clarifying the requirements relating to system processing and data.

The following points should be considered when producing a Requirements Prototype at this stage:

- ensure that the requirements relating to processing and data have been obtained as comprehensively as possible, before any prototypes are developed, and that they are documented in the Requirements Catalogue

- since the objective is to define requirements rather than produce a solution, it is possible to prototype with a completely different environment from that envisaged in the proposed system. For example, it would be reasonable to use a spreadsheet to model calculations that may eventually be embedded in a transaction processing system

- identify the requirements that are still unclear or need a deeper level of definition, which seem good candidates for prototyping to clarify and add detail to them

Chapter 6
SSADM and prototyping

- consider which users should be involved in the interactive sessions and to which requirements they can contribute. Consider also which developers should be involved

- determine what type of prototype should be built. Typically, it should concentrate on the detail of processing and data used

- set a time and effort limit within which the prototyping process must take place. Ensure that the Stage plan covers the necessary activities and effort.

Interface with SSADM

Potential input products to Requirements Prototyping in this module are:

- Prototyping Scope
- Required system DFM
- Requirements Catalogue
- Data Catalogue
- Required system LDM
- Selected BSO
- User Catalogue.

Requirements Prototyping is carried out as an addition to Step 310, Define Required System Processing, following definition of the logical model in the conventional manner as far as possible. It should also be preceded by data modelling in Step 320, Develop Required Data Model, as far as required for the prototype.

Products

The key products are:

- Prototyping Scope including the preliminary scope and definition of each function prototyped. The scope is an input to the prototyping process. Following prototyping, however, it is a valuable output to record the actual scope of what was done

Prototyping in an SSADM Environment

- application products from the prototype itself, including data used and processing definition in some form

- Prototype Result Log containing the user reactions to the prototyping sessions.

Following Requirements Prototyping, information from the activity is incorporated into SSADM products, primarily:

- Requirements Catalogue
- Required system LDM
- User Catalogue
- Data Catalogue
- DFDs plus supporting Elementary Process Descriptions for the required system.

6.3.2 Specification Prototyping (RS)

Specification Prototyping requires more substantial preparation than the types of prototyping used in the earlier stages of SSADM. In particular, the following is important:

- sufficient analysis must have been carried out to define the functions to be prototyped, including production of relevant Effect Correspondence Diagrams (ECDs) and Dialogue Designs

- a full Prototyping Scope should be produced giving all functions to be prototyped

- choice of tool affects the extent of the prototype that can be easily built, for example, to provide navigation between screens

- the prototype need not necessarily be built in the target environment, providing that there is confidence the results can be incorporated successfully into the specification. For example, the dialogues and screens must be translatable into the likely technical environment as envisaged in the preferred Feasibility Study composite option

Chapter 6
SSADM and prototyping

- a decision must be made on how to treat data accessing in the prototype, that is, does it need to be simulated? will hard coding suffice? or is it necessary to access tables? This rests on the importance of data accessing to the specification at this stage. It should be borne in mind that physical accessing is not formally designed until Stage 6 of SSADM

- a Prototyping Plan must be produced, as covered in Section 5.3, Management of prototyping. The plan must cover the timescale, activities, resources and products to be produced from prototyping and is an integral part of the Stage plan for Stage 3

- the initial prototype must be adequately tested with test data supplied by users using formal test plans, to prevent failures when exercising the prototype

- as the prototype is likely to be reasonably detailed in terms of its functionality, users who are to exercise it must be supplied with adequate explanatory documentation

- in contrast with the prototyping used in the earlier stages, Specification Prototyping is formally iterative. After each exercise of the prototype, the prototype should be assessed regarding its objectives, and a decision made as to the relative benefit of another iteration, considering the timescale and effort constraints.

Figure 9 shows the prototyping cycle for Specification Prototyping.

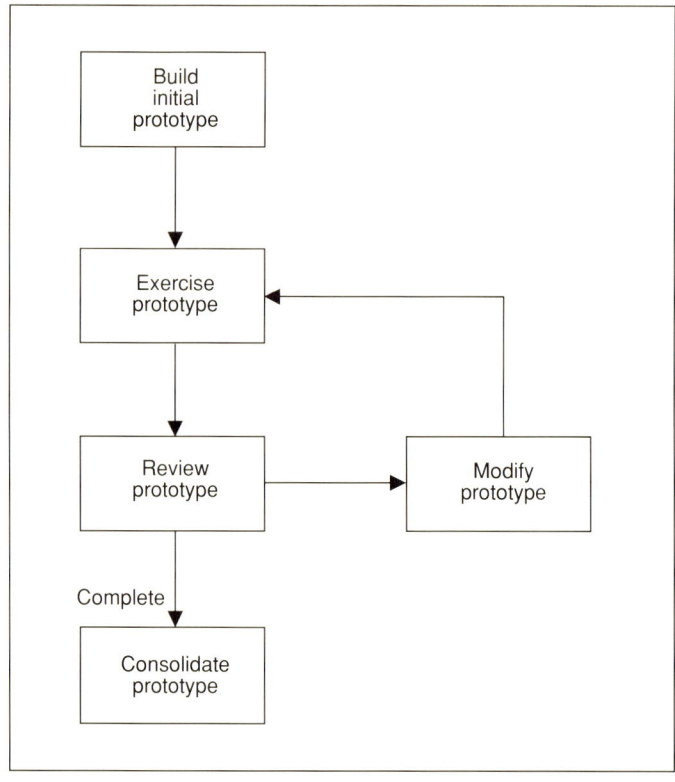

Figure 9: Specification Prototyping cycle

SSADM interface

Potential input products to Specification Prototyping are:

- Prototyping Scope
- Requirements Catalogue
- Required system LDM
- Data Catalogue
- User Catalogue
- User Role/Function Matrix
- I/O Structures
- initial Function Definitions.

Chapter 6
SSADM and prototyping

Specification Prototyping is carried out in Step 350, Develop Specification Prototypes.

Products

The key products are:

- application products from the prototype, typically prototyped dialogues, defining screens, screen processing, navigation and possibly data accessing

- Prototype Result Log containing the user reactions to the prototyping sessions.

These are used to update the following SSADM products:

- Required system LDM
- User Role/Function Matrix
- I/O Structures
- Data Catalogue
- Entity Life Histories (ELHs) and ECDs
- Function Definitions.

6.4 Logical System Specification module

Figure 10 shows suggested types of prototyping for use in the Logical System Specification module.

Prototyping in an SSADM Environment

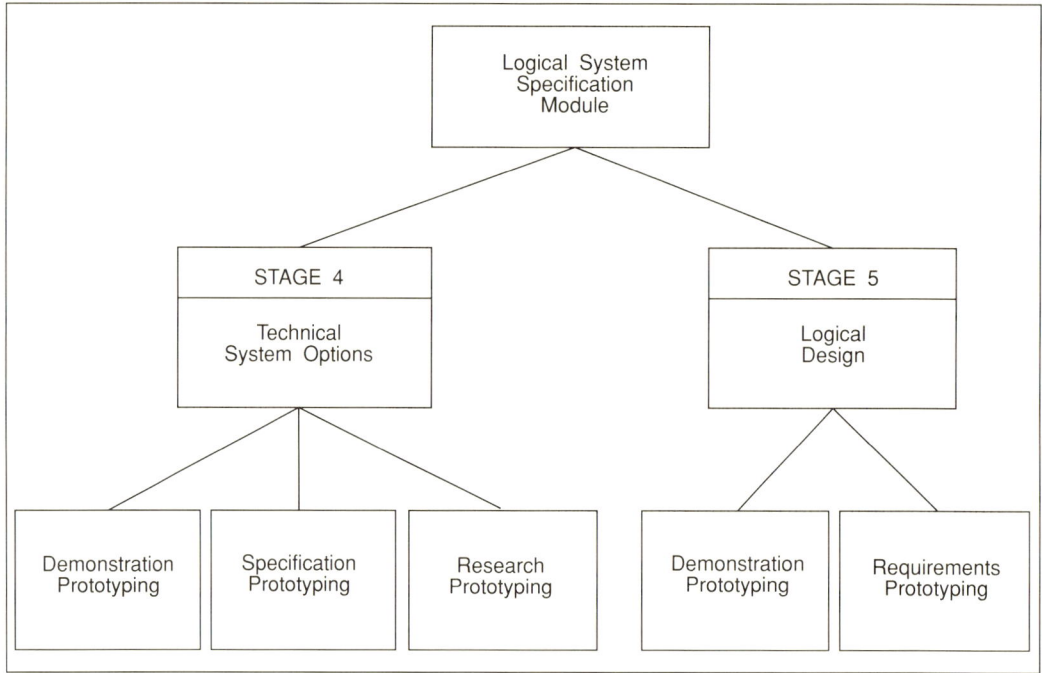

Figure 10: Prototyping types in Logical System Specification module

6.4.1 Demonstration prototyping - technical system options

A Demonstration Prototype would be built to illustrate one or more TSOs that have been already defined. Generally, the TSOs reflect alternative ways of implementing similar functionality. In this context, a prototype can be invaluable in demonstrating the essential differences between implementations.

The following guidelines should be considered when producing a Demonstration Prototype for TSO presentation:

- each option to be prototyped must be clearly defined before any attempt is made to build a prototype

- the prototype for each option must be consistent with the target environment, as this is a key aspect of the decision-making process

Chapter 6
SSADM and prototyping

- decide how the prototype is to be used, either in informal discussions with users or as a demonstration to the Project Board before the formal End-Stage Assessment meeting takes place. This influences the nature of the prototype to be built
- test the prototype sufficiently to ensure it is robust enough for the demonstration
- produce a list of the issues that are expected to be resolved by demonstrating the prototype and ensure that the demonstration covers these.

Interface with SSADM

The prototype(s) should reflect one or more of the TSOs produced in Step 410, Define Technical System Options. Inputs to the prototyping process are:

- Prototyping Scope
- System Description from TSO
- BSO
- Requirement Specification products, particularly:
    - Processing Specification
    - Data Catalogue
    - Function Definitions.

The prototype is not a substitute for the defined TSO.

Products

All decisions and information resulting from the demonstration of the prototype must be fed back into the relevant TSO.

A variety of feedback is possible since the prototype could cover various aspects of the TSO. For example, feedback could be obtained on:

- overall hardware/software environment
- performance
- ease of use
- look and feel

- security
- capacity
- functionality
- interfaces.

6.4.2 Specification prototyping - technical system options

A Specification Prototype can be built to model one or more TSOs. The objective is to define those TSOs, or parts of them, in more depth than may be possible with paper specifications. The TSOs show alternative ways of implementing similar functionality and the Specification Prototype concentrates on the nature of those implementations.

For example, there may be two TSOs that deliver similar functionality; one based on a new database design, whilst the other makes use of existing physical data structures. It may be useful to build a specification prototype for one or both of them to assist in the definition of the option, for example, its performance, ease of use and security aspects.

The following guidelines should be considered when producing a Specification Prototype for TSO definition:

- consider the use of any Specification Prototype produced in the RS module as a start point for this prototype. *In most cases it is not worth developing a Specification Prototype specifically for the definition of TSOs.* This is because the activity is geared specifically to choosing the optimum TSO, with unnecessary detail being avoided

- a Specification Prototype should only be built if there is a clear possibility of producing usable outputs, which can be incorporated into the TSO and ultimately into the Logical Design. If this is not so, consider whether a Demonstration Prototype might be more appropriate

- decide on the scope of the prototype. If it tends to concentrate on narrow issues rather than the TSO as a whole, perhaps a Research Prototype would be more appropriate

Chapter 6
SSADM and prototyping

- each TSO to be prototyped must be scoped and defined as far as possible before any attempt is made to build a prototype

- the prototype for each TSO must be consistent with the target environment, as this is a key aspect of the decision-making process

- a Prototyping Plan must be produced, as described in Chapter 5, Management of prototyping. The plan must cover the timescale, activities, resources and products to be produced from prototyping and is an integral part of the Stage plan for Stage 4

- the initial prototype must be adequately tested, with test data supplied by users and, using formal test plans, to prevent failures when exercising the prototype

- Specification Prototyping is an iterative process. After each exercise of the prototype, its objectives should be assessed, and a decision made as to the relative benefit of another iteration, considering the timescale and effort constraints

- the Specification Prototype may be extended to cover User Dialogues in detail, after the TSO has been chosen.

Interface with SSADM

The prototype(s) should reflect one or more of the TSOs produced in Step 410, Define Technical System Options. Inputs to the prototyping process are:

- Prototyping Scope

- System Description from TSO

- BSO

- Requirement Specification products, particularly:

    - Processing Specification

    - Data Catalogue

    - Function Definitions

    - Specification Prototype.

63

| | | The prototype is not a substitute for the defined TSO. |

Products — All information resulting from the prototype must be fed back into the relevant TSO.

6.4.3 Research prototyping - technical systems options

The use of Research Prototyping in this module is focused on a specific technical issue related to the implementation of the system in the environment. There are many potential aspects that could benefit from prototyping.

The following guidelines should be considered when producing a Research Prototype in this module:

- ensure that there is a clear benefit to be gained from Research Prototyping by considering:
    - what aspect of the implementation cannot be resolved by normal means of analysis? For example, producing a prototype to prove the performance of a data design may take much longer than working out the performance from a theoretical model
    - what lessons do the development team want to learn from the proposed prototype and are they able to quantify the results?
    - who is the target reviewer for the prototype? Does the prototype enable the reviewer to make a decision that could not be reached by other means?
- care should be taken to assess the effort required to be put into prototyping at this point and ensure that it is not out of proportion with the total effort required to produce the TSOs. For example, producing a prototype of a Graphical User Interface (GUI) may take a lot of effort with existing tools and if a TSO using that approach is not chosen the work may be wasted
- conversely, it may be that the Research Prototype has application for more than one project and this should be considered in determining its viability

Chapter 6
SSADM and prototyping

- normally Research Prototyping does not require iterations of a review cycle. Research Prototyping must have clear objectives and the prototype must be able to be checked readily against those objectives.

Interface with SSADM

The Research Prototype is produced before TSOs are selected. There must be time to assimilate the results from the Prototype into the relevant TSO(s).

Inputs to the prototyping process are:

- Prototyping Scope
- Outline Required Environment Description from FS
- RS products, particularly:
  - Processing Specification
  - Data Catalogue
  - Function Definitions.

Products

The results of the Research Prototype, including reviewer's assessment, are included in the System Description and Technical Environment Description for the relevant TSO(s).

For example, if the prototype concerned distributed data and a communications link, then the distributed data results would be included in the System Description, and the communications link results would be included in the Technical Environment Description.

In this context, 'results' are the viability, efficiency, performance etc of the technical approach taken by the prototype and highlights the key differences between the prototype functionality and the TSO.

6.4.4 Demonstration prototyping - logical design

The following guidelines should be noted when producing a prototype to demonstrate User Dialogues:

- the prototype should include a menu structure, if it is easy to set one up with the prototyping tool. However, it may not be worth-while for purely demonstration purposes unless the structure is very important to the development or likely to be controversial. Also consider whether the structure developed for prototyping purposes can be automatically documented and easily incorporated into the Logical Design product

- decide on the level of detail which needs to be demonstrated. This means, for example, deciding on whether the screens should contain all required items or only key ones

- consider whether all aspects of the dialogues need to be demonstrated, for example, whether exceptional routes through the dialogue should be included or only the main ones

- decide whether ancillary facilities such as help screens need to be included. At this point, help screens are useful at the dialogue level, but are less likely to be needed at the screen level

- the demonstration prototype dialogues need not include data accessing. The data may be hard-coded or read in from a parameter file to give the appearance of data access

- screen formats are not required to be designed in detail until the Physical Design module is reached. Any formats designed for prototyping purposes are equivalent to logical groupings of dialogue elements (LGDEs) and provide useful input to the later design process, but cannot be assumed to be final. Care must therefore be taken to ensure that any changes subsequently made to what has been demonstrated by the prototype are agreed with the user

Chapter 6
SSADM and prototyping

- the demonstration prototype is within the chosen TSO and should obey the technical constraints of that option. However, it is not essential for the prototype to be in the same technical environment.

Interface with SSADM

The Demonstration prototype is built during Step 510, Define User Dialogues and demonstrated at the end of this step to confirm the acceptability of the dialogues with representative users.

Main inputs to the prototyping process are:

- Prototyping Scope
- Function Definitions, a dialogue is normally an implementation of a function
- I/O Structures
- Requirements Catalogue
- Installation Style Guide and any standard formats
- User Role/Function Matrix.

Products

The output from the demonstration prototype is incorporated into the standard SSADM products, including:

- Menu Structure, probably produced prior to the prototype
- Command Structure generated from the prototype, if possible
- Dialogue Structures
- Dialogue Element Descriptions
- Dialogue Control Tables
- Dialogue Level Help
- Requirements Catalogue updates.

The practitioner may prefer to build these products in parallel with the prototype.

6.4.5 Requirements prototyping - logical design

The following guidelines should be noted when producing a Requirements Prototype for User Dialogues:

- normally the prototype includes a menu structure if it is easy to set one up with the tool. This is useful if the structure can be changed as part of the requirements elucidation process

- decide on the level of detail which needs to be demonstrated. This means, for example, deciding whether the screens should contain all required items or only key ones. Detail need only be provided where there is a real possibility of participating users being able to take decisions at this level

- initially the dialogues need only contain the main or default paths

- decide whether ancillary facilities such as help screens need to be included. Help screens at the dialogue level are useful at this point, but those at the screen level are not needed initially. The Requirements Prototyping process should help to indicate the nature of help required at the more detailed level

- normally the Requirements Prototype dialogues need not include data accessing, the data may be hard-coded or read in from a parameter file to give the appearance of data access

- screen formats are not required to be designed in detail until the Physical Design module. The initial formats designed are commented on by users as part of the process and this provides useful input to the later design process. Care must be taken to ensure that any changes subsequently made are agreed with the user

- the Requirements Prototype at this point is within the chosen TSO and should obey the technical constraints of that option. However, it is not essential for the prototype to be in the same technical environment.

Chapter 6
SSADM and prototyping

Interface with SSADM	The Requirements Prototype is built during Step 510, Define User Dialogues. It is used during this step to build up comprehensive dialogues that take account of detailed user requirements.

Main inputs to the prototyping process are:

- Prototyping Scope
- Function Definitions, a dialogue is normally an implementation of a function
- I/O structures
- Requirements Catalogue
- Installation Style Guide and any standard formats
- relevant industry standards
- User Role/Function Matrix.

Products	The output from the Requirements Prototype is incorporated into the standard SSADM products, including:

- Menu Structure, probably produced prior to the prototype
- Command structure generated from the prototype, if possible
- Dialogue Structures
- Dialogue Element Descriptions
- Dialogue Control Tables
- Dialogue Level Help
- Requirements Catalogue updates.

The practitioner may prefer to build these products in parallel with the prototype.

Annex A Possible prototyping tools

A.1	**Data dictionary/ Repositories**	This is ideally a repository for many of the logical level SSADM products, including the LDM, Logical Data Flow Model, Logical Data Store/Entity Cross Reference and all components of the Requirements Catalogue. However, not all dictionaries operate well, or at all, at the logical level.

At the physical level, data dictionaries hold the definitions of files, records, data items and physical processes. They may sometimes include all the run-time components as well.

Contribution to prototyping

The logical aspect of the dictionary helps by ensuring consistency of the entries made and producing cross-references, for example, of data and process. This helps Specification Prototyping, for example, by assisting the accurate definition of the logical view, before embarking on any prototyping.

In the prototyping process itself, the data dictionary sometimes facilitates the transition from logical to physical, for example, by producing first cut database schemas from logical data designs.

When designing prototype screens, the data dictionary may store the screen definition, including its data items, and may cross-reference screen data items to attributes in the data model.

Features to look for

The following are useful features for prototyping:

- holds definitions of a wide variety of logical level products
- holds definitions of a wide variety of physical level products including screens
- generates physical products from logical ones, such as database from data model
- same dictionary usable by all development tools, that is, enquiry facility, report generator, 4GL

- ability to hold data validation rules, again to prevent having to duplicate the definitions
- support for security definitions such as access privileges
- support for version control.

Annex A
Possible prototyping tools

A.2 Fourth generation languages (4GLs)

A 4GL provides a means of defining physical processing in a concise manner, usually in a non-procedural way. Usually it takes away some of the complexity of handling screens or windows and databases/files by providing special facilities. The emphasis is on being able to generate physical processes quicker and with fewer errors. There is often some deterioration in performance compared with a conventional language (3GL).

There are many different 4GLs and the range of facilities offered varies enormously, so it is important to check the specific features of the intended 4GL.

Contribution to prototyping

This can range from the ability to construct screen layouts quickly, to process definition, to data access modelling, to whole dialogue production. 4GLs are one of the main tool types that make prototyping a viable proposition.

Without a 4GL, it is often not practical to prototype.

Features to look for

The following features are found to be useful in most forms of prototyping:

- screen painting, including item definition, validation and editing

- close integration of screen item definition with data item definitions in the database

- non-procedural process definition. If it is procedural, it should be at a high level

- screen and window handling facilities

- support for repeating lines, such as repeated sequence of detailed records related to a master

- menu definition and processing facilities

- database/file access facilities and which database systems are supported

- dialogue definition and navigation facilities, preferably under developer control as opposed to being standardised

- automatic generation of maintenance screen information for each defined table. This saves a lot of time in coding and is useful for sample/test data entry
- ready-made dialogue templates
- rapid amendment cycle, for example, able to partially regenerate the prototype rather than regenerate the whole, after partial amendments
- recognition of data model constraints, such as referential integrity support
- exits to a 3GL may be useful for some prototypes.

Annex A
Possible prototyping tools

A.3 **Relational database**   This is a DBMS which implements data definitions expressed in relational form. The important feature for prototyping purposes is the ability of the DBMS to implement the LDM in physical terms with the minimum of translation. Having done this, it is relatively simple to change since the physical model generally consists of a collection of two-dimensional tables.

Contribution to prototyping

Where a prototype involves the need to model data accessing, then a relational database is ideal. It can also be useful even just to supply data to simple screen layouts and dialogues, provided the means of accessing it, such as by a 4GL, is relatively simple.

Features to look for

The following features prove useful in a prototyping context:

- ease of setting up and modifying tables
- ability to reflect the user's perception of the data
- ease of generation of indexes
- version control for different prototype versions
- ease of access from the chosen 4GL
- integration with data dictionary enables changes to be made at the logical level and translated through to the physical design, so that the logical design does not get out of step with the prototype
- ability to define business rules as part of the physical data design, which cuts down the need for procedural code and makes the prototype construction quicker and more predictable.

Many relational databases in the market are bundled with 4GL features. It is advisable to check these 4GL features against the desirable features for 4GLs listed in section A.2.

A.4	Screen painters	Sometimes stand-alone screen definition tools are available, separately from 4GLs. The tools enable definition of screens in an interactive mode, giving the developer the facility to position fields and text on the screen in a WYSIWYG fashion. Usually, this is supplemented by the ability to define the field contents, formatting, editing, and validation characteristics. The defined screen can then be called, for example, by a 4GL.
	Contribution to prototyping	Screen painters are useful for Demonstration Prototyping, Requirements Prototyping and even Specification Prototyping. Screen painters do not normally define the whole dialogue. They are normally useful, however, to define menus.
	Features to look for	The following features prove useful for prototyping:

- ability to handle necessary devices
- screens callable, for example, from a 4GL
- screens re-usable in the real system
- support for repeating lines, for example, from multiple detail records associated with a master
- ease of change
- ability to produce hard copy/documentation.

Annex A
Possible prototyping tools

A.5 Enquiry languages These are similar to 4GLs except that they are specialised for the extraction of data from databases or files and for the production of screens or reports.

Contribution to prototyping They are useful throughout prototyping, for the same reasons as 4GLs, but only where the requirement is for an enquiry process.

Features to look for The following features prove useful for prototyping:

- Query by Example, where the enquiry can be set up on the required output form
- transparency to the format of files/databases being accessed
- ability to integrate with other aspects of the application in some cases
- storage of defined enquiries
- flexibility in terms of manipulating data
- flexibility in terms of output formats.

A.6 Report generators

These are essentially similar to Enquiry Languages, but are specialised to generate output reports and not enquiry screens.

Contribution to prototyping

They are useful specifically for the purpose of demonstrating reports. A report generator may often be useful where data usage is being prototyped, that is, the developers are trying to establish the data requirements.

Features to look for

This is basically the same set as for Enquiry Languages, plus:

- ability to generate to screen or print as required
- ability to produce complex reports, such as matrix style reports, where cross referencing of totals is required.

Annex A
Possible prototyping tools

A.7   **Code generators**   Code generators are like 4GLs in that they allow physical processes to be defined quicker and with less errors. The difference is that, whatever the start point of process definition, which may be diagrams, or may be some kind of high level code, the result is generated in 3GL code, which can then be compiled in the normal way. A 4GL normally generates executable code, or is interpreted.

Contribution to prototyping

The place of Code Generation in prototyping is a difficult one, because it is generally found to be too cumbersome a process for prototyping purposes. It is unlikely to be very useful for Requirements or Demonstration Prototyping, but may just be usable for Specification Prototyping, provided that the number of iterations is kept under strict control.

Features to look for

The features which would make code generation a feasible proposition for prototyping are:

- incremental generation, that is, not necessary to regenerate the whole system if a change is made

- good screen definition and handling. This is less likely to be found in a code generator than in a 4GL

- data manipulation facilities.

A.8 Upper CASE tools

This covers CASE tools which provide analysis and design facilities and their associated repositories of information. The repository aspect has been covered under Data Dictionaries.

Contribution to prototyping

As with Data Dictionaries, the logical analysis supported by the tool often helps by ensuring consistency of the entries made, and producing cross-references, for example, of data and process. This helps Specification Prototyping, for example, by assisting the accurate definition of the logical view before embarking on any prototyping.

Beyond this, the actual use of the tool in producing prototype screens, dialogues or process definitions is often very limited compared with a 4GL.

Features to look for

A more direct contribution to prototyping may be achieved for tools which provide:

- logical screen definitions
- logical dialogue definitions.

Some CASE tools include 4GL features such as screen painting and report generation.

Annex A
Possible prototyping tools

A.9 **Lower CASE tools** This covers CASE tools which provide design and construction facilities, and their associated repositories of information. The repository aspect has been covered under Data Dictionaries.

In practice there is frequently an overlap with upper CASE tools, that is, the same product often covers both functions.

Contribution to prototyping The lower CASE tool usually helps to ease the transition from logical to physical design. It is primarily aimed at producing the complete system rather than a prototype. It is often too detailed and time-consuming to use as a prototyping mechanism. It should be considered for Specification Prototyping only.

Features to look for For prototyping purposes, the lower CASE tool typically provides:

- detailed process definition facilities, for example, by means of pseudo-code, structure diagrams etc
- physical data design facilities, for example, by translation from logical design, plus ability to define extra features
- expression and testing of access paths
- code generation in some tools usually based on high level code or structure diagrams
- screen and dialogue definition.

A.10	**5th generation languages and extensions**	This covers languages such as Prolog and LISP and extensions such as Frame systems. These are included as potential providers of prototyping facilities because they enable the definition of processing in non-procedural terms. Prolog can be used to model complex logic in processes, by expressing the business rules that apply. Frame systems can be used to define common logic and where it is used or inherited.
	Contribution to prototyping	These tools are applicable to Research Prototyping, for example, to find out whether a process can be built to perform certain logic. Alternatively, they might be used in Requirements Prototyping to explore what the user wants the system to do.
	Features to look for	There are no specific features which need to be singled out for prototyping purposes. Clearly, the use of such tools is not recommended unless the development team have familiarity with this technology and can see a clearly defined purpose for it.

Annex A
Possible prototyping tools

A.11 Shells (Expert System Shells, Object Shells)

A Shell is defined as a ready-made template or environment which shapes the application or business transaction. There are varied types, such as 4GL templates for specific kinds of transaction, Expert System Shells which provide a framework in which knowledge-based applications can be built and Object Shells in which object-oriented applications can be built.

A Shell enables the business function to be built quicker than with standard development tools, at the price of having to fit the function within the constraints of the Shell. This may, for example, constrain the formatting of screens, the way data can be processed and the overall shape of the dialogue.

Contribution to prototyping

Use can be made of a Shell in Demonstration, Requirements or Specification Prototyping. It is important that the user understands there may be a large difference between the prototype and the eventual system, given that the system is not actually implemented in the Shell.

Features to look for

The use of such Shells should be limited to the applications where the Shell has some specifically useful feature to offer. For example, it may be identified that the Shell provides the form of dialogue that is required, and can therefore save a significant proportion of the initial construction effort.

Annex B Estimating approaches

Bottom-up estimation

It is essential to produce a detailed list of activities in order to get a realistic estimate. The overall activities may be taken from the following set:

- determine scope of prototype
- plan prototyping activity
- build initial prototype
- test prototype
- prepare prototyping environment
- review prototype with user
- assess user feedback
- revise prototype
- produce Prototyping Report.

Each of these activities needs to be broken down to a greater level of detail. For example, *Build Initial Prototype* consists of a number of identifiable activities such as screen design, data design and so on. The level of breakdown depends on the type of prototype, where within SSADM the prototype is being developed and the extent of the prototype.

The overall estimate for the prototyping activity is then based on the individual estimates of all the constituent activities. However, care must be taken to allow for the timescales within which the activities need to take place, such as prototyping review sessions where allowance may need to be made for user availability.

Estimating by analogy

There are clear benefits to be found if there are metrics from previous prototyping projects from which to judge the effort and timescale. This may be particularly applicable when trying to judge the impact of a number of iterations of the prototyping process.

Metrics from previous projects are only useful if they include measures of the prototype itself as well as the effort required, such as how many functions, screens, dialogues, etc were produced. It would also be necessary to record what type of prototyping took place and how many users were involved.

Constraint models
Normally prototyping is undertaken within strict time, budget and resource constraints. It may be useful to see what prototyping can be justified in a development and to decide the level of coverage that can be achieved in the prototype in terms of functions, user roles etc. The effect of planning this way is to concentrate on what it is essential to achieve and find out.

Product based estimation
A complementary method to activity estimation is to use a measure of the prototype products to be produced and relate this to the likely effort - a simplified form of Function Point estimating. Refer to the companion volume *Estimating Using MKII Function Point Analysis* for more details.

The benefit of this method is that it forces the estimator to think about what is to be produced.

Contingency
Certain activities in prototyping are inherently uncertain in terms of effort and/or timescale and need a larger than average contingency to be applied. This applies to reviewing the prototype with the user and the consequent activities of assessment and revision as it is difficult to predict what the user reaction will be and what its consequences are.

A further uncertainty is how many iterations of the prototype may be necessary. It is essential to plan a specific timescale and to have a specific maximum number of iterations in mind. However this does not remove the possible need to make tactical revisions depending on how the sessions go.

As later activities in the development depend on the results of prototyping, it is essential to plan sensibly by having some contingency to compensate for this uncertainty.

Annex B
Estimating approaches

Metrics

To improve the accuracy of estimating for prototyping, it is essential to provide feedback of hard information from the experience of the installation. A number of basic metrics are suggested and outlined:

- type of prototype
- SSADM module
- number of functions prototyped
- number of dialogues
- number of screens
- number of data items - on screens
- number of levels of menu - when prototyped
- number of users in sessions on first and second iterations
- user hours in sessions
- development effort - initial prototype, including testing
- number of review sessions and average duration.

Bibliography

SSADM documentation	The SSADM Version 4 Reference Manual is published by NCC Blackwell Ltd and is available from NCC Blackwell Ltd, 108 Cowley Road, Oxford OX4 1JF.
	ISBN 1 85554 004 5
ISE Library	The Information Systems Engineering Library volumes, published by CCTA, are available from HMSO Bookshops. A number of volumes on SSADM topics have been published and others are in preparation. ISE Library volumes are available from HMSO Publications Centre, PO Box 276, London SW8 5DT.
	The following volume is referenced in this publication:
	Estimating Using MKII Function Point Analysis
	ISBN 0 11 3305788
Information Systems Guide	The Information Systems Guides, published by CCTA, are available from John Wiley & Sons Ltd, Baffins Lane, Chichester PO19 1UD.
	The following guide has topics referenced in this publication:
	B8 Systems Engineering
	ISBN 0 471 92533 0
PRINCE documentation	The PRINCE Reference Manual is published by NCC Blackwell Ltd and is available from NCC Blackwell Ltd, 108 Cowley Road, Oxford OX4 1JF.
ITIL	The IT Infrastructure Library is available from HMSO bookshops or from HMSO Publications Centre, PO Box 276, London, SW8 5DT
	Change Management
	ISBN 0 11 330525 7

Glossary

Business System Options (BSOs)
The aim is to take the Requirements Catalogue, Current Services Description and User Catalogue and use this information as the basis on which to decide the most appropriate way for the development to meet the business needs.

CASE tool
A Computer Aided Software Engineering tool. This is a tool which supports the application of development techniques during the SSADM modules, such as Logical Data Modelling or Data Flow Diagraming. Most CASE tools also provide an integrated repository which holds the information recorded on the objects, for example entities, and normally provide facilities for reporting on the information and providing integrity checks.

A distinction is often made between Upper and Lower CASE tools which may be distinguished:

- Upper CASE tools support analysis and specification of systems at the logical level, in SSADM terms, modules FS, RA, RS, LS
- Lower CASE tools support design and construction of systems, in SSADM terms, module PD.

CASE tools sometimes span both of these areas.

Code Generator
A software tool which enables the definition of processing in a high level manner, sometimes non-procedurally, and generates 3GL code, such as COBOL, from the high level script. Some code generators may generate code from a combination of diagrams, such as data flow diagrams and data model diagrams, and process specifications produced at the logical level.

Command Structure
This product shows the directions that control can take when a user decides to complete or terminate a particular dialogue. This allows navigation to be implemented with or without menus in dialogues.

Current Services Description	Provides the details of the logical current system which, with the Requirements Catalogue and User Catalogue, is output from Stage 1: Investigation of Current Environment.
Database Management System (DBMS)	A system that enables the definition and maintenance of physical databases and provides facilities for application processes to access the data. The data is organised in a database in a logical manner to facilitate access by the applications. The precise organisation varies according to the database architecture supported; hierarchical, network or relational.
Data Catalogue	The central repository for all the descriptive information about items of data. This includes physical details which may be found during data flow modelling activities as well as physical design activities. Logical data modelling provides information about attributes, the logical equivalent to data items.
Data Dictionary	A computer database which contains the definition of system objects, primarily data definitions, and includes accessing facilities to its definitions. The definitions may include both logical definitions, such as entities and attributes, and physical definitions, such as databases, files, records. The dictionary may contain also process definitions at logical and physical levels and other objects such as screen definitions. Some dictionaries contain links between these definitions.
Data Flow Diagrams (DFDs)	Show how services are organised and processing is undertaken. It should be a simple, readily understood diagram that can act as an effective means of communication between analysts and users.
Data Flow Model	A set of Data Flow Diagrams and their associated documentation. The diagrams form a hierarchy with the Data Flow Diagram Level 1 showing the scope of the system and the lower level diagrams expanding the detail as appropriate. Additional documentation provides a description of the processes, input/output data flows and external entities.

Glossary

dialogue
The on-line activity required by a particular user role so that they can action a particular function.

Dialogue Control Table
This product is used to identify and capture the navigation between the logical groupings of dialogue elements under normal conditions. This table also details the different order in which particular aspects of the dialogue may be undertaken.

dialogue element
A section of an input or output data flow which may consist of many data items. Each dialogue element is represented as a box on a Dialogue Structure.

Dialogue Element Descriptions
A product used to describe a dialogue element. A set of these provides the detailed documentation for a Dialogue Structure.

Dialogue Level Help
A product that is used to detail the level of help that the user/user role requires to progress through this dialogue.

Dialogue Structures
This product gives a diagrammatic representation of a dialogue. Each box on the Dialogue Structure equates to a dialogue element. Input/output operations are allocated to dialogue elements.

Effect Correspondence Diagram (ECD)
Shows all the effects an event has on data within the system and how those effects impact upon each other. ECDs provide the access path details for update functions which are used in logical design activities.

Elementary Process Descriptions
A product used to describe the business environment in which the process is trying to operate. A requirement for common processing may also be described within an Elementary Process Description and cross-referenced to the elementary processes or functions using it.

Enquiry Language
A language which facilitates the production of screen enquiries, and possibly also reports. Usually it provides reasonably English-like commands to express the retrieval requirement. It may obey a recognised standard such as ANSI Structured Query Language (SQL).

entity	Is something, whether concrete or abstract, which is important to the area of business being investigated. Logical data modelling identifies types of entity not individual occurrences, that is Tenant and Applicant not John Smith.
Entity Descriptions	Documents all the details concerned with an entity on the Logical Data Structure, including details of state indicators applied during entity life history analysis. There are associated Relationship Descriptions for each related entity on the Logical Data Structure.
Entity Life Histories (ELHs)	These are structure diagrams for all Entity Life Histories identified within the system. An ELH is a structure combining all possible lives of every possible occurrence of the entity.
Feasibility Study module (FS)	The Module whose objective is to produce the Feasibility Report which suggests the way ahead for the project. The activities form a short assessment of a proposed information system to determine whether the system is feasible and appropriate to the business needs of the organisation. Feasibility is assessed in terms of the managerial, business, financial, technological and cultural needs of the organisations.
Fifth Generation Language (5GL)	A language which supports artificial intelligence processing, such as rule-based processing. Prime examples are Prolog, based on logic statements, and LISP.
Fourth Generation Language (4GL)	A language which defines processing in a high-level and usually non-procedural way. It typically takes far fewer statements to express the same processing as for instance, COBOL, and usually achieves this by providing special facilities for handling screens and data. Some 4GLs operate from diagrammatic input such as structure charts and data models.
Frame System	A method of organising processing in a hierarchical manner, which supports rule processing, and facilitates the definition and use of common logic by inheritance.
function	A set of system processing which the users wish to schedule together, to support their business activity.

Glossary

Function Definition
Is the description of the function and provides a cross-reference to other associated SSADM products.

Graphical User Interface (GUI)
A user interface which makes use of graphical objects, such as icons, for selection of options and usually has a windowing capability, enabling multiple window displays on the same screen.

Implementation Prototyping
A type of prototyping which produces a prototype that can be carried forward, albeit with some modification, as the working system.

I/O Structure
Documents the input to and outputs from a function, or part of a function.

Installation Style Guide
Is a set of standards about the nature, approach and style of the human factors aspects of computerised systems. The standards should be followed by all projects undertaken within an organisation.

Logical Data Flow Model
Is produced during logicalisation in Stage 1 (Step 150). It combines the existing services and the desired processing requirements, removing all physical considerations.

Logical Data Model (LDM)
Provides an accurate model of the information requirements of all or part of an organisation. This serves as a basis for file and database design, but is independent of any specific implementation technique or product. The LDM consists of a Logical Data Structure, Entity Descriptions and Relationship Descriptions. Associated descriptions of attributes/data items and grouped domains are maintained in the Data Catalogue.

Logical Data Store/ Entity Cross Reference
Is a matrix showing the correspondence between logical data stores in the Data Flow Model and the entities on the LDM. This ensures that a main data store corresponds to an entity or group of entities. Each entity on the LDM must be held completely within one main data store. Transient data stores are not included on this matrix.

Logical Data Structure
A diagrammatic representation of the information needs of an organisation in the form of entities and the important business relationship between them.

logical grouping of dialogue elements (LGDE)
Dialogue elements within a particular Dialogue Structure are grouped together where input/output requirements suggest that there are benefits to be gained, such as simpler processing.

Logical System Specification (LSS)
The Module product from the Logical System Specification module which consists of the Selected TSO, the Technical Environment Description and the Logical Design.

Menu Structure
A product that provides a diagrammatic representation of the menus to be used within the system.

Metric
A formula which measures a specific characteristic of a product or process. The product may be an SSADM product, such as a LDM, and the process may be a system development process such as Prototyping. Metrics usually measure cost, quality or productivity.

mock-up
A prototype which simulates the system in some way giving the appearance of a working system, but not using the real system facilities or architecture. For example, a text processor may be used to give the appearance of a screen format.

non-procedural
A means of expressing processing in terms of requirements, without having to define the order in which the processing must be executed.

Outline Required Environment Description
A brief description of the requirements to be included within the proposed system. Produced during the Feasibility Study. The analysis reflects that carried out in Stage 1, but is not completed to the same level of detail.

Processing Specification
The Step Product from Step 360: Develop Processing Specification. This product is not shown explicitly on the SSADM structural model. It exists to identify the quality criteria associated with the close links between entity-event modelling results and the products being input to this Step. Development of this product may identify errors in other products and force previous Steps to be revisited.

Glossary

Product Breakdown Structure — Identifies the products which are required and which must be produced by a project. This document describes the system in a hierarchic way, decomposing it through a number of levels down to the components of each product.

Prototype Result Log — Used to record the results of the prototype demonstration. This document is used in a similar capacity to minutes of a meeting. Each request made by the user is documented on the log, with a change grade, and the log is updated later to show what changes are required.

Prototype Scope — Is used by the project board to define the boundaries and objectives for the prototyping activities.

Prototype Session — The meeting in which a prototype is demonstrated to the users and feedback is obtained. It may vary from a formal to informal meeting in size and duration, depending on the objectives and the type of prototyping being undertaken.

Prototyping — The building and demonstration of a working model of a system, or part of a system, to communicate with users and verify logical results.

Relationship Descriptions — Documents the details of a relationship between two entities on the Logical Data Structure.

Report Generator — A software tool which facilitates the definition of reports from defined data. It obviates the need to code procedurally and may allow the definition of reports in a WYSIWYG fashion using the screen as a report template.

Required System Logical Data Model — Provides the detail of the proposed system information requirements. It is developed during the Requirements Specification and Logical System Specification Modules.

Requirements Analysis module (RA) — The objective is to produce the Analysis of Requirements. Within this, the Selected Business Option defines the scope of further investigation.

Requirements Catalogue	Is the central repository for information covering all identified requirements, both functional and non-functional. Each entry is textual and describes a required facility or feature of the proposed system.
Requirements Specification module (RS)	The objective is to produce the Requirements Specification.
Screen Painter	A software tool which enables the interactive definition of screen contents and layout, by means of the developer positioning the fields and text on the screen and entering appropriate definitions. The screen definition is then stored in a format suitable for processing by a language or 4GL.
Selected Business System Option	This is a description of a chosen system development direction. The description documents the system boundary, inputs, outputs and the transformation taking place within the boundary. Essentially the description is textual with supporting annotated elements from the Current Services Description.
Shell	A ready-made template for a dialogue or piece of processing, within which part of an application can be constructed. This usually obviates much of the work of construction, at the price of constraining the design within the bounds of the Shell. This is a separate concept from the user interface part of an operating system, which is also termed a shell.
state indicators	State indicators are used as an expression of the structure of an ELH, in a format which is used during the Logical Design Stage to enforce the defined sequence of events. A state indicator should be thought of as an additional attribute within each entity.
System Description	Shows how the RS is met by the Technical Environment Description for a particular TSO. In many cases, the major decisions in this area have already been taken in choosing a BSO.
Technical Environment Description (TED)	Provides the specification of the technical environment which is produced once the TSO has been selected. This detail is then passed on to physical design activities.

Glossary

Technical System Options (TSOs)	The set of TSOs which has been developed so that the system development direction can be chosen. Each option documents the function to be incorporated and details implementation requirements. Each description is textual with some planning information. Functional elements are taken directly from the RS.
User Catalogue	Provides a description of the on-line users of the proposed system. It includes details of job titles and the tasks undertaken by each of the identified users.
user role	A user role is defined as a collection of job holders who share a large proportion of common tasks.
User Role/Function Matrix	Dialogues are identified as being the cross-reference between user roles and on-line functions. The matrix maps correspondence between function and user roles, thus identifying these dialogues. Reading down from the user roles axis provides the initial Menu Structure for the system.
workshop	A structured meeting in which participation is sought to resolve issues or make decisions. The workshop is led by a workshop leader or facilitator and concentrates on a well defined subject area, within a strict time limit, for example, two hours. Workshops can be used as part of the process to resolve requirements, and may benefit from the incorporation of prototype demonstrations as part of the workshop.
WYSIWYG	An acronym for 'What you see is what you get'. This is an attribute of tools such as screen painters, where the act of building the screen is carried out by direct manipulation of the screen as it is presented to the user. As applied to report generators, WYSIWYG means that the report is printed exactly as it appears on the screen.

Prototyping in an SSADM Environment